Families

Editor: Danielle Lobban

Volume 417

independence
educational publishers

First published by Independence Educational Publishers

The Studio, High Green

Great Shelford

Cambridge CB22 5EG

England

© Independence 2023

ISBN-13: 978 1 86168 877 4

Printed in Great Britain

Zenith Print Group

Acknowledgements

The publisher is grateful for permission to reproduce the material in this book. While every care has been taken to trace and acknowledge copyright, the publisher tenders its apology for any accidental infringement or where copyright has proved untraceable. The publisher would be pleased to come to a suitable arrangement in any such case with the rightful owner.

The material reproduced in **issues** books is provided as an educational resource only. The views, opinions and information contained within reprinted material in **issues** books do not necessarily represent those of Independence Educational Publishers and its employees.

Images

Cover image courtesy of iStock. All other images courtesy of Freepik, Pixabay and Unsplash.

Additional acknowledgements

With thanks to the Independence team: Shelley Baldry, Tracy Biram, Klaudia Sommer and Jackie Staines.

Danielle Lobban

Cambridge, January 2023

Contents

Introduction

Families is Volume 417 in the issues series. The aim of the series is to offer current, diverse information about important issues in our world, from a UK perspective.

About Families

Family life in the UK has changed considerably in the past few decades. In this book we explore what makes a family, how the definitions of family have changed and the importance of family units.

Our sources

Titles in the issues series are designed to function as educational resource books, providing a balanced overview of a specific subject.

The information in our books is comprised of facts, articles and opinions from many different sources, including:

- Newspaper reports and opinion pieces
- Website factsheets
- Magazine and journal articles
- Statistics and surveys
- Government reports
- Literature from special interest groups.

A note on critical evaluation

Because the information reprinted here is from a number of different sources, readers should bear in mind the origin of the text and whether the source is likely to have a particular bias when presenting information (or when conducting their research). It is hoped that, as you read about the many aspects of the issues explored in this book, you will critically evaluate the information presented.

It is important that you decide whether you are being presented with facts or opinions. Does the writer give a biased or unbiased report? If an opinion is being expressed, do you agree with the writer? Is there potential bias to the 'facts' or statistics behind an article?

Activities

Throughout this book, you will find a selection of assignments and activities designed to help you engage with the articles you have been reading and to explore your own opinions. Some tasks will take longer than others and there is a mixture of design, writing and research-based activities that you can complete alone or in a group.

Further research

At the end of each article we have listed its source and a website that you can visit if you would like to conduct your own research. Please remember to critically evaluate any sources that you consult and consider whether the information you are viewing is accurate and unbiased.

Issues Online

The **issues** series of books is complimented by our online resource, issuesonline.co.uk

On the Issues Online website you will find a wealth of information, covering over 70 topics, to support the PSHE and RSE curriculum.

Why Issues Online?

Researching a topic? Issues Online is the best place to start for...

Librarians

Issues Online is an essential tool for librarians: feel confident you are signposting safe, reliable, user-friendly online resources to students and teaching staff alike. We provide multi-user concurrent access, so no waiting around for another student to finish with a resource. Issues Online also provides FREE downloadable posters for your shelf/wall/ table displays.

Teachers

Issues Online is an ideal resource for lesson planning, inspiring lively debate in class and setting lessons and homework tasks.

Our accessible, engaging content helps deepen student's knowledge, promotes critical thinking and develops independent learning skills.

Issues Online saves precious preparation time. We wade through the wealth of material on the internet to filter the best quality, most relevant and up-to-date information you need to start exploring a topic.

Our carefully selected, balanced content presents an overview and insight into each topic from a variety of sources and viewpoints.

Students

Issues Online is designed to support your studies in a broad range of topics, particularly social issues relevant to young people today.

Thousands of articles, statistics and infographs instantly available to help you with research and assignments.

With 24/7 access using the powerful Algolia search system, you can find relevant information quickly, easily and safely anytime from your laptop, tablet or smartphone, in class or at home.

Visit issuesonline.co.uk to find out more!

What does 'Family' mean to parents and children?

An excerpt from Family Life Survey annex to 'Family and its Protective Effect: Part 1 of the Independent Family Review'.

Which words were associated with family?

When asked which three words respondents first thought of when they heard the word 'family', parents and children across all ages, gender and ethnicities were likely to select similar words of positive sentiment. 'Loving' was the word most likely to be selected by parents (64%), followed by 'home' (43%), 'caring' (40%), 'supportive' (38%) and 'happy' (37%). All of the negative terms listed in the survey (stressful, struggles, pressure, breakdown, unhealthy and unsupportive) were selected by fewer than 7% of parents. Similarly, when asked to select three words to describe family, children (aged 8-17) were most likely to select 'loving' (63%), followed by 'happy' (51%) and 'home' (48%).

'Happy', 'supportive' and 'loving' were most likely to be selected together by both parents and children. 'Happy' and 'loving' were most likely to be selected together, both of which frequently linked to many of the other positively oriented words such as 'stable' and 'supportive'. 'Caring' was also linked to 'stressful' and 'pressure'. Compared to the children who answered this question, parents' word choices were more varied as most words, regardless of sentiment, linked to multiple other words. For example, 'stressful' links to 'loving', 'unsupportive' and 'pressure'.

What does family mean to children and parents?

Both parents and children (aged 8-17) were also asked 'Please tell us, in your own words, what family means to you'.

Parents

Thematic analysis of 1000 responses from parents revealed the following key themes, listed in order of relative occurrence.

1. Everything/life/purpose
2. Love/care/joy
3. Support/trust
4. Safety/security/stability
5. Unit/nuclear/biological – includes descriptions of the family unit
6. Togetherness/ time together
7. Memories
8. Stress/worry/responsibility (including financial worries)
9. Disappointment
10. Children's futures (including being a good role model)
11. Health and loss
12. Lack of support/negative relationships

References to family being 'everything', 'my world' or 'life' was the most commonly mentioned theme by parents. Many of these responses also talked about love, a feeling of being cared for and supported by family.

'My three daughters are my world. I wish they lived with me.' – Dad, 55

'Family is everything to me, to me family are people you love unconditionally and they feel the same. I have a few, yet very close, friends who I would also consider family although they don't share blood. Family is support, love, non-judgmental and what I personally need to remain sane. I wouldn't be me without family, and I most definitely would not be happy.' – Mum, 25

'Family is everything to me. Knowing that every morning I wake up next to my loving wife, I get to cuddle and kiss my sweetest children… That is all I ever wanted. And a stable income. However, family is also a lot of work, commitment and compromise.' – Dad, 42

Another theme that emerged from this question was the idea of a family unit. This theme included responses describing the members of their family, and how family could span across multiple households and generations.

'It's complicated. I adore my husband and son, but our son is disabled and life is full of battles. I win most of them, but they're still battles, and I wish I didn't have to fight every day for what some families take for granted. I love my dad, but I'm one of the sandwich generation who is trying to raise a family and keep a parent healthy and independent, and I'm darned tired… I am mostly happy, and I appreciate I am very lucky, but things are hard sometimes.' – Mum, 52

'Married couple with man and woman only and children after marriage. Stable loving home life that work through problems together. Woman looks after home and children, man goes to work and earns the money. Proper traditional family values that are strict but fair.' – Mum, 49

However, many parents also recognised that their family extended beyond their relatives, but to friends, community members and those with a shared history or bond.

'As humans we require support emotionally, physically and much more from our families. Family is not necessarily blood bound.' – Dad, 35

'Family means providing emotional, financial and moral support to the people I love, no matter what.' – Mum, 44

Many parents also mentioned the importance of safety, security, stability and a sense of trust in those they consider part of their family.

'A very supportive resource that have a wealth of experience and are willing to help us at anything time.' – Dad, 44

'Family means being there for one another and being patient with the children and always meeting their needs' – Mum, 27

Parents often emphasised the importance of spending time together, creating memories a sense of togetherness.

'Family to me means spending time together doing things we love with everyone we love. Creating awesome memories!' – Mum, 43

'Family means that we share our lives together, good times and bad. We listen, we laugh, we argue, we forgive, we communicate. Family for me is warm, caring and protective. My children are safe when we're together. Family means creating a super strong support hub that lasts a lifetime.' – Mum, 51

Cutting across many of these themes was a sense of responsibility as a parent, not only for their children, but also for their parents, which often linked to worries or stress regarding other aspect of life, including finances, housework and other relationships. Likewise, children were sometimes mentioned as the care giver to a parent or sibling, taking on some or all of the responsibilities that would traditionally be left to parents.

'Family means providing emotional, financial and moral support to the people I love, no matter what.' – Mum, 56

'Families cause a lot of stress. Especially with money worries and feeling of guilt when you don't feel you can offer enough time and support to each child…. Sometimes one child causes a lot of emotional upset and stress, and this means you feel you neglect other children in the home. Children are a constant worry and I think every parent worries about their child's safety constantly…' – Mum, 49

'My children are my family they are the most loving supportive daughters anyone could ask for. My youngest daughter 27 is my full-time carer, and has given up so much for me. My 16-year-old son is a real handful at times, he has autism and puts a lot of pressure on the family as a whole he has severe anger issues and frequent melt downs. We also have 5 dogs that I love nearly as much as my children. I have always told my children that if they ever have any problems however had I am always here and I will always support and help as much as possible.' – Mum, 52

Parents of children with SEND were especially likely to talk about the importance of family, alongside the pressures and strains of family life.

'My family is the most crazy, loving, supporting family. Lockdown brought us so much closer as we struggled mentally and physically! Have a non-verbal, autistic son with global delay and sensory issues can be difficult. He requires care from me 24 hours a day. It's essential to have strategies and support from family during these hard times with him. Also, having a 3-month-old, working, everyday house chores, shopping, coping with money and costs rising. So important to stick together.' – Mum, 28

'My family (husband and two children, plus three cats) are the foundation of the safety of my home…. It's been hard adapting to my daughter being away socialising sometimes as much as half the week, but it makes it more special when she's here. Family beyond those who live in my house are stressful and best taken in small doses.' – Mum, 45

Children

Thematic analysis of over 600 responses (children aged 8-17) indicates the following key recurrent themes, ordered by relative frequency of mentions (includes only themes that have been mentioned more than 5 times):

1. Love and kindness
2. Unit – includes references and descriptions of the family unit
3. Care/help/looked after
4. Support and communication
5. Everything
6. Security and safety
7. Happy
8. Fun/activities/holidays
9. Togetherness/time together
10. Stress and annoying

Children were most likely to give responses relating to the love when asked what family means to them were also frequently mentioned themes by children, as well as being looked after or helped by their family members.

'I love my Mummy.' – Boy, 8

'Family means someone who loves you and somewhere that's warm and loving.' – Girl, 8

Many children gave descriptions of family structure, such as a list of those who they would consider 'in their family' and those who are outside their sense of family.

'Your family is your parents and your brothers and sisters and other relatives which you love and they love you.' – Girl, 13

'Mum and dad and my brother. Also, my Nan and Grandpa and my uncles. Looking after me.' – Boy, 8

'Family is mummy, she looks after me and I know she loves me even if my dad does not. I don't need my dad I just need my mummy because she is the best. She is kind and gives me lots of cuddles. She tells me I can do anything I want to if I work hard for it. She let me go to the high school I want to not just the nearest one, so I get a good education.' - Girl, 11

Many children also mentioned pets as part of their family, as well as friends and members of their wider community.

'My mum is autistic like me and worries. Mum has a best friend that is family too. We have a cat...she is family. Mum takes me on holiday. We went to Iceland. Iceland horses and a blue lagoon. She takes me to see trains which is my favourite.' – Boy, 8

'I love family time and when we play lots of games. Me and my sister argue a lot and that sometimes makes my mum mad at us, but we are sisters what does she expect. I like our home and our pets...they are lovely and...my sister's hamster is in her room and he smells funny but it is our family.' – Girl, 13

'Family is the group of people who make me feel accepted, loved, safe and supported. They don't have to be blood related. My friends are like family too.' – Girl, 17

Some children specifically mentioned that their family was separated or lived across multiple households. Some also mentioned hoping to see more of their extended family.

'I have a blended family. I have step-family and half siblings but my family is full of love.' – Prefer not to say, 14

'My mum and my dad. They live apart now so I have 2 homes, but my family is mum and dad.' – Boy, 13

'Live with mum and boyfriend, 2 brothers one side one brother the other, split family but it works OK now.' – Boy, 15

'My family are my mum and sister who I live with and then my dad and my other sister, so I have two sets of parents who live apart then I also have my grandparents and uncles and an aunt.' – Girl, 17

'My family is my parents and brother and my grandparents. I wish we would see our grandparents more though.' – Boy, 16

Care and a feeling of being 'looked after' were also frequently mentioned themes by children, as well as being helped by their family members.

'Family is me and my mam, she is always there for me. I have autism and other health issues and she is by my side through all the struggles I have.' – Boy, 13

'My sister and my mum looking after me and making me happy and making sure I have nice food' – Boy, 11

Similar to the responses from parents, children

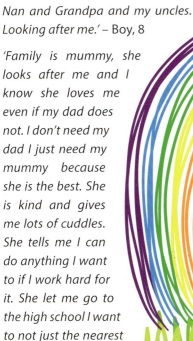

Write

Write a paragraph on what family means to you. it doesn't have to be about your own situation, if you prefer you can write about how you think a family should be.

often referred to family being 'everything', 'my world' or 'life'.

'My family mean the world to me. They mean knowing I always have someone to love and care for me and supporting me in everything I do. They give me confidence make me feel happy and good about myself.' – Girl, 12

Many children mentioned a sense of trust, acceptance and communication within their family and how important that is to them. For example, children said they were often able to talk to their family members about any problems they might have and recognised that other children were less able to talk to their families.

'I know if I have a problem there's always someone in the family I can speak to. I have a couple of friends at school whose home life is a bit rubbish as their parents take drugs. I'm so glad Mum isn't like that. Dad was a bit, but he left, and we never see him.' – Boy, 17

'To me it means having someone to love you unconditionally in spite of you and your shortcomings. Family is loving and supporting one another even when it's not easy to do so. It's being the best person you could be so that you may inspire your loved ones. Family doesn't see colour, race, creed not culture it sees heart.' – Boy, 17

Children also told us about the hardships facing their family, how these issues affect their family life and how they support each other during these times.

'After Mum's death, Dad and I carried on together, just as a smaller family than before, sharing the duties as I got older.' – Boy, 17

'It's only me and my mum because my waste of space dad never bothered with us when he was here...now he's gone it's so much better! Family should be the ones who are there for you no matter what. I've made lots of stupid teenage mistakes, but my mum always helps me through them and she's always there for me and puts me first even when I don't want her to. She's the stability and feeling of feeling secure and unjudging. I just wish we had more money so mum wouldn't have to worry so much, and we could spend more time together.' – Boy, 15

'I think I have a good family. We argue sometimes but we all love each other. Sometimes it is hard as we can't afford much things but my mum and dad always try and make sure we have everything. Family holidays are my favourite memories.' – Boy, 17

Older teenagers or children of families with older children sometimes mentioned their expectation for their family to let them grow up, give them space or leave home, or that they missed their older siblings who had left home.

'It's my mum, dad, and brother first and foremost. I've got cousins, grandparents too but mum and dad are my first family links. Family is about getting on, support, sometimes arguments, but also letting go as I grow up...' – Girl, 16

'I like my family, we have fun most of the time, even though I argue with my brother and like being on holiday together. I miss my sister who is at university.' – Boy, 17

September 2022

The modern family: how the notion of family has evolved

The concept of family is not the 2.4 nuclear picture we saw a century ago. In the modern world, family means different things to different people.

How we view family life has changed and evolved dramatically. In today's society, families come in all shapes, sizes and dynamics and this week, we wanted to take a closer look at the evolution.

What's driven the change?

A number of factors have contributed to the making of today's modern family. From higher divorce rates, fluctuations in the number of people getting married and those choosing to cohabit, to changing attitudes to the nuclear family dynamic.

Since 1981 the number of marriages every year has fallen by a third. According to the Office for National Statistics, fewer people are getting married than at any time in more than 100 years. But while marriage is decreasing, that doesn't mean families are; the family dynamic has just changed. We're seeing more families with unmarried parents, but still living together and working together in the same way a married couple would.

The legalisation of gay marriage has also made an impact, making each family unit unique and with its own particular experiences.

The role of grandparents

Nowadays, more women are in the workplace than ever before. As of June 2020, the Office for National Statistics recorded 72.7% of women aged 16-64 were employed,

a 52.8% increase from 1971. As a result, in many families both parents work full-time. This has meant that the role of grandparents as carers for the children has increased over the past few decades.

Longer life expectancy has also played its part. A recent survey suggests 2.2 million people will live in multi-generational homes in the UK by 2025. Grandparents now make up a large portion of the population, and in many families they become caregivers to their grandchildren.

This shift in dynamic has meant that divorce or separation has a bigger impact on grandparents than it perhaps would have had in previous years, and we talk more about this in a previous blog.

Divorce and step-parents

In the first decade of the 20th century, there was just one divorce for every 450 marriages. Between then and now, attitudes towards divorce have changed. And so too has the independence and rights of women.

Today, the divorce rate is much higher. In 1971, the number of divorces was 50,000 per year. In 1981, that figure increased to 150,000.

With higher divorce rates come different family dynamics: stepparents, blended families and single parent families, all of which have become much more common. Family, from an emotional viewpoint, has become less about biology. It's about who people live with, share experiences with and who they form deeper connections with.

Single parent families

In the UK there are around 1.8 million single parents, which makes up nearly a quarter of families with dependent children. There are many reasons behind the rise in single parent families. But one thing is for certain; it's one reason why grandparents may play a bigger role in family life as carers, as single parents may have to go to work and need support in looking after the children.

7 June 2021

Key Facts

- 2.2 million people will live in multi generational homes in the UK by 2025.

- Since 1981 the number of marriages every year has fallen by a third.

www.thestartingpointcentre.co.uk

Families and households in the UK

- In 2021, there were 19.3 million families in the UK, which represents a 6.5% increase over the decade from 2011 to 2021.

- In 2021, there were 3.0 million lone parent families, which accounts for 15.4% of families in the UK; the proportions ranged from 13.1% in the South East of England to 17.8% in the North East of England.

- The number of families that include a couple in a legally registered partnership in the UK has increased by 3.7% in the past decade, to 12.7 million; by comparison, the number of cohabiting couple families saw an increase of 22.9% over the same period, to 3.6 million.

- There were an estimated 28.1 million households in the UK in 2021, an increase of 6.3% over the last 10 years.

Table 1: Families by family type and presence of children, United Kingdom, 1996 to 2021

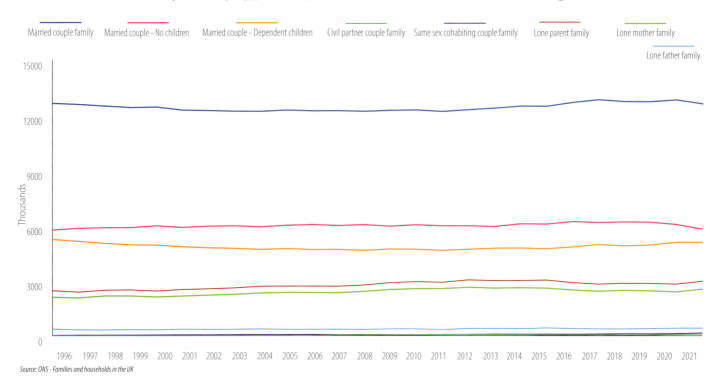

Source: ONS - Families and households in the UK

Table 2: People in families by number of children, United Kingdom, 1996 to 2021

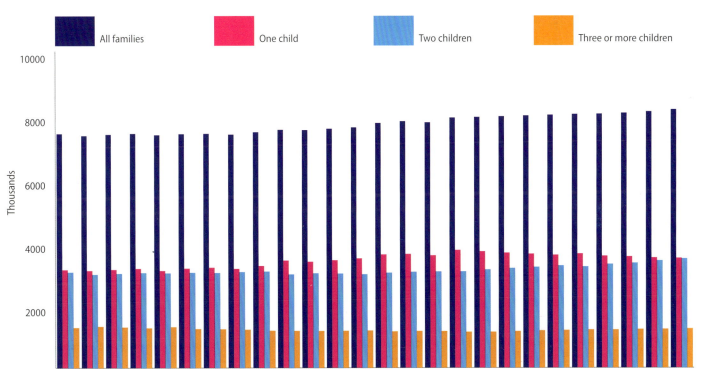

■ All families ■ One child ■ Two children ■ Three or more children

Source: ONS - Families and households in the UK

- The number of people living alone in the UK has increased by 8.3% over the last 10 years; in 2021, the proportion of one-person households ranged from 25.8% in London to 36.0% in Scotland.

- In 2021, 3.6 million people aged 20 to 34 years were living at home with their parents; this represents 28% of people in this age group, an increase from 24% a decade ago.

9 March 2022

Research

Create a questionnaire to find out about family sizes of your classmates. How many only children are there? Are there many with more than three siblings? Present your findings in a graph.

What does the modern family look like?

An excerpt from *Family Life Survey annex to 'Family and its Protective Effect: Part 1 of the Independent Family Review'*.

Household composition

The parent and child sample used for these analyses is nationally representative for the UK by oldest child's age, gender, household region and parental employment status. The adults without children sample is weighted by adult age and gender.

Adults who are parents

On average, family households across the UK have two adults (2.0 adults in England and Scotland, 2.1 in Wales and 1.9 in Northern Ireland, this includes any adult, not restricted to parents). Across all households in this sample, 16% reported including one adult, 72% had two adults, 8% had three adults within the household. The largest number of adults living with the responding parent in this sample was six adults (n=5).

Most parents were either married (60%), co-habiting (20%) or civil partnered (1%) and also listed a married husband or wife (57%) or co-habiting partner (19%) as the second adult living within their household. A much smaller percentage listed a son or daughter (3.2%) and or parent (2.6%) as the second adult living in the household.

The survey was boosted to ensure representation for parents from ethnic minority groups. Just over 8 in 10 of parents that responded to the survey were White (83%), 7% were Asian, 5% were Black and 4% were of mixed or other ethnic backgrounds.

Adults without children

Households of adults without children in the UK comprised of, on average, 1.7 adults (slightly lower than for parents). Similar proportions of adults without children lived alone (42%) or with one other adult (46%) and 8% of adults lived with two other adults. Forty three percent of adults without children were single, 23% were married, 17% were co-habiting and 7% were divorced. The remaining 10% of adults without children were, together but living apart (5%), widowed (3%) or civil partnered (2%). Three quarters of adults without children identified as heterosexual (75%), 10% as lesbian or gay, 4% as bisexual and 1% as another sexual orientation.

Children

Across the UK, households with children had on average 1.6 children living in the household at the time of the survey.

Figure 1. Number of parents or guardians living with the child at their main home.

Note: Households with 3 or more parents or guardians living with the child(ren) at their main home were removed due to small sample sizes.

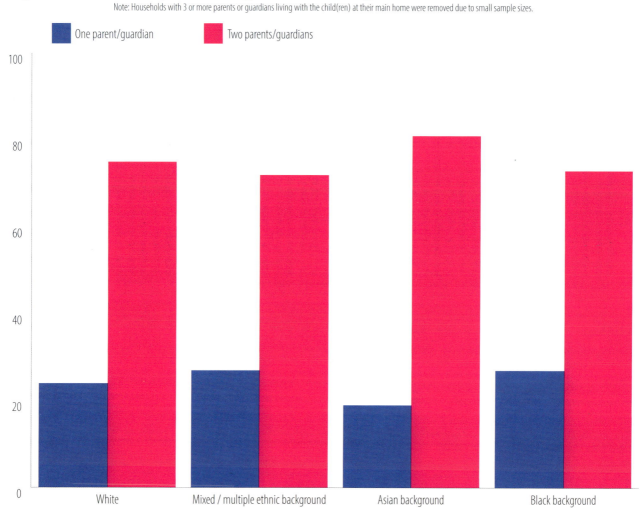

Source: Children's Commissioner

Table 1. Number and percentage of children within each age group that had a parent that did not live at the child's primary address.

Child age group (years)	Children with a parent not at their main address	
	Sample size	Percent of age group (%)
0-3	124	18
4-7	180	24
8-11	219	28
12-14	153	29
15-17	153	28

Source: Children's Commissioner

The highest number of children (under 18) listed as living in the same household as the parent responding to the survey was 7. The majority of relationships between the responding parent and the children in the household were parental, either a son or daughter, or stepson or stepdaughter.

The average number of children per household in England was 1.6. This was lower than in Wales (1.9) and Northern Ireland (1.8), while Scotland had the lowest average of children per household, in line with London (both 1.5).

The number of children per household varied significantly by ethnic group. Respondents with mixed or multiple ethnic group backgrounds (n=86) or Asian backgrounds (n=246) both had on average 1.8 children per household, and 55% of households had 2 or more children, while respondents from Black backgrounds (n=165) had 1.6 children on average, 45% of households with 2 or more children.

Lone parent households and having a parent not residing at their child's main home

Across the UK, 16% of parents (n=518) reported to be the only adult in a household, yet nearly a quarter of all parents reported to be a lone parent or guardian (24%). By comparison, 42% of adults without children reported to live alone.

The proportion of parents reporting to be a lone parent varied by age of parent, rurality of household. Parents in the 16-24 age groups were most likely to be a lone parent (40%), but this was a small sample size and therefore should be seen as an indicative finding (n=49). Parents in urban areas were more likely than rural or sub-urban parents to be lone parents (urban = 29%, sub-urban = 21%, rural = 23% lone parents).

The proportion of lone parent households was lower for respondents from Asian backgrounds (19%) and higher for respondents from Black backgrounds and those from Mixed/Multiple ethnic backgrounds.

A quarter of children in this survey (equivalent to 2 million children in the UK +/- 140,000) had a parent or parents that did not reside at their main address. Older children (age 8-17) were significantly more likely to have parents not residing at their main address, compared to children aged 0-7. A more detailed breakdown of the proportion of children with a parent not living at their main address can be found in Table 1.

Children in London were most likely to have a parent not residing at their main address (30%), while children in the South West of England were least likely (17%). Despite this, there were no significant differences between rural and urban areas (both 27%). However, this was lower for children living in sub-urban areas (22%).

September 2022

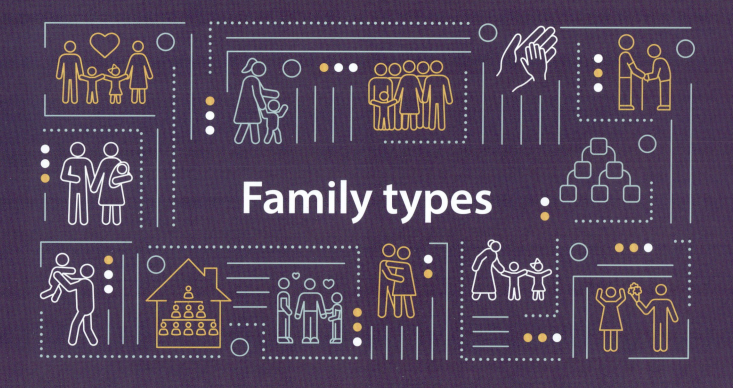

Family types

What is a family unit? The basic definition is a group of individuals, residing together who are related by birth, marriage or adoption.

Over time the family unit has changed considerably, from the nuclear family in the 50's we now have a multitude of family types which we will discuss below. Some families will fit into more than one family type. It is impossible to list all the forms of family, but here we look at six different types.

Nuclear family

Nuclear families, often known as a traditional family, consist of two parents and one or more children. Whilst this used to be two opposite-sex parents, it now includes same-sex parents.

The parents are in a committed relationship and either married or unmarried. The nuclear family was thought to be the most universal type of family unit, however, this has changed over the past few decades. Also, with the falling fertility rate, the number of children has reduced to 1.7 children per family. However, we are surrounded by images of two parents with two children as the 'ideal' family, but this is now an outdated view as families become more diverse.

The nuclear family became more common in the industrial revolution, when people moved away from small towns and villages to cities for work. Previously, families lived in an extended form, either in the same house or street. They lived and worked very close by, often all the family members working in the same profession, such as farming. The move away from villages meant that families became smaller, and more self-contained. It also meant that mothers were expected to stay at home and look after the children and the house.

Extended family

An extended family is when more than two generations of a family live together. For example; grandparents, parents and children. This form of family is common around the world, especially in Asia, where people are more likely to support their elderly family members so they can stay at home rather than going into care homes. In the UK however, this used to be a common family type, but there was a shift in the 20th century to the nuclear family. People are starting to shift back towards the extended family though, due to a number of factors, such as, an ageing population and preferring to look after family members who need more support in their old age, increasing property prices, which mean that many can not afford to move out of their family home, or a breakdown of a relationship, where they have to return to their parents home.

Extended families do have some benefits such as increased social support, including childcare and care for the elderly.

Single parent family

Single parent families consist of one parent, who is either never married, divorced, widowed or by choice, who has one or more children. Single parent families started to become more common in the 1960's when societal changes meant that some of the stigmas of being a lone parent began to change. The Divorce Reform Act 1969 made divorce easier, as people could end a marriage without having to prove fault, and marriages could be ended after separation of two years, if both parties desired divorce, or five years if only one party desired divorce.

This meant that many people who had not been able to easily divorce, could now do so, and so led to an increase in single parent families.

However, the number of single parent families is now at similar levels to the 1990's - despite a peak of 26% in 2012 - in 2020 it fell to 21.6%.

Blended family

The blended family, also known as stepfamily, is when two separate families merge into one. This can happen for example, when two divorced parents marry or move in together, or when someone with a child marries a person without children and they then go on to have children together.

The blended family is becoming increasingly common, and perhaps this is why the number of single parent families has dropped?

Creating a blended family can have some problems however. It can be difficult to adjust to differing parenting styles, having inconsistences between the resident and non-resident parents and having to build relationships with step-parents, step-siblings or step-children. Jealousy can be a problem between step-siblings - which can sometimes cause a rift between the parent and step-parent. Everyone knows the trope of the wicked stepmother, trying to ruin the lives of her step-children, this though, only happens in fairytales! Relationships aren't always successful though in blended families as sometimes people just do not get on. It can take a lot of work and perseverance to have a successful blended family, just as it can with any other family type.

Mindmap

Can you think of any other types of family? Create a mindmap with types of families and include strengths and weaknesses for each type.

Design

Design your family tree. Include as many of your family as you know. How many branches of your tree do you think there will be?

Blended families can work very well, children have additional adults that they can build a strong relationship with, that is different to the typical parent-child relationship. Also, they can gain additional sets of grandparents, aunts, uncles and cousins.

Childless family

A childless family is one without children living in the home. This may also be an 'empty nest' family where the children have left the family home and either moved away, or created their own family unit. It can also be couples that could not, or decided not to, have children.

A childless family is usually a couple in a committed relationship who live together. This can be an opposite-sex, or same-sex couple.

Conclusion

In conclusion, all families are unique and your family may fit into more than one of these categories, or none at all. There is no right or wrong family type. The family types listed here are just a small selection of the types of family there are, and your family type is as unique as you are.

You may even consider friends to be like family, and that is okay too. Just because you are related to someone does not guarantee that you will love, or even like them. Not all families are happy, sometimes relationships can be strained. As the saying goes 'you can choose your friends, but you can't choose your family'.

January 2023

Over half of children in England and Wales are now born to unmarried parents – overturning a history of stigma and discrimination

An article from The Conversation.

By Kate Gibson, Leverhulme Early Career Fellow in History, University of Manchester

In 2021, more babies – 51% – were born to unmarried mothers in England and Wales than to those in a marriage or civil partnership for the first time since records began in 1845. This is a huge change. For centuries, 'illegitimacy' and unmarried parenthood has been associated with stigma, shame and disadvantage.

The civil registration of births only began in 1845, but we have parish register data that goes back to the 16th century. Although it fluctuated, the 'illegitimacy ratio' – the proportion of births marked as to unmarried parents in parish registers – never passed 7% of the total from the 16th century until the 1960s. Since then, however, the proportion has climbed steadily.

This increase shows not only that more babies are being born to parents who are not married, but that fewer parents are hiding the circumstances of their children's birth. The illegitimacy ratio represents only those children whose birth to unmarried parents was noticed by the state, so the real number would have been much higher.

Many parents altered birth dates, used false names or pretended to be married to prevent the stigma of illegitimacy being attached to their children's birth record for life.

People born to parents who were not married to each other have been legally discriminated against in many cultures across the world for centuries. In England and Wales, laws to deter and punish illegitimacy existed from at least the early medieval period.

This reflected Christian beliefs that sex outside marriage was sinful. It was combined with the need to ensure political and economic stability in a society where property, status and identity was based on inheritance from father to child.

Facing stigma

Biological paternity could not be proven in a time before DNA testing, so the theory was that marriage gave men security that a child was theirs. Without marriage, paternity rested on a woman's word, which was considered dubious in a society that feared female sexual power.

Due to these fears, there was very little demand for reform. It was only in 1987 that the legal distinction between legitimate and illegitimate was finally eradicated.

There were small reforms improving the legal rights of children born to unmarried parents from 1926 onwards, but their position was always worse than that of a child whose parents were married. An illegitimate child born before 1987 was judged to have no legal father, which affected their rights to inherit property.

In the centuries before the welfare state, children's entitlement to state support was contested. In a society

largely set up for households supported by a male breadwinner or a dual income, children born to unmarried parents were more likely to grow up poor.

My research shows that these children in the 18th century were more likely to be separated from their parents and moved between different foster households while they were growing up, and more likely to feel excluded from their communities.

This stigma did not improve into the 20th century. Historians have found that well into the 1970s, illegitimacy was seen as deeply shameful. Families often hid the circumstances of their children's birth out of fear that they would be bullied as 'bastards'. The impact of this secrecy had long-term effects on children's identity and self-esteem.

Unmarried mothers continued to find it difficult to get work and maintenance payments for their children throughout the 20th century. Before 1977, for example, unmarried mothers and their children were usually excluded from council housing lists. This sent a strong message that unmarried parents should be blamed and penalised for their supposed bad decisions.

However, the story is not one of unrelenting disadvantage. Many parents and their children were helped by their families and neighbours, and many children grew up in loving homes. It is hard to escape, though, the fact that any support always took place against the backdrop of legal hostility towards their children's very existence. They lived within a system that continually argued that unmarried families were inferior.

It is amazing, then, that in just 35 years, England and Wales have gone from legal stigma to almost complete acceptance of equality between children born to parents who are married and those who are not.

Foundations of change

Reforms in the divorce law and the de-criminalisation of same-sex relationships have steadily eroded the idea that political and economic stability depends on the traditional model of the heterosexual married couple and their children. The development of reliable, affordable DNA paternity tests means that the central social rationale behind illegitimacy discrimination – the impossibility of proving paternity – has now disappeared.

Changes in the opportunities available to women have also considerably mitigated the impact of single motherhood. Women are able to earn more now than at any point in the past. Access to contraception and abortion means that couples now have much more control over when they become parents.

This progress is uneven, though. Many countries around the world still seek to regulate female sexuality and reproduction, and religious or conservative organisations continue to argue that marriage is the central foundation of society.

The history of illegitimacy shows that cultural and legal change is possible. But sexual and reproductive freedom is only a relatively recent phenomenon, and more work is needed to combat the legacy of centuries of discrimination.

24 August 2022

THE CONVERSATION

www.theconversation.com

Children flourish in new forms of family, but some still suffer outsiders' stigmatisation

Many want schools to challenge prejudice against new family forms and want parents to provide more information about donors, half-siblings, and surrogates, according to a new book, *We Are Family*.

By Susan Golombok

People concerned about children growing up in new forms of families (e.g., LBGTQ families, families created by donor eggs) have worried unnecessarily. In the face of dire warnings about such families, studies consistently show that their children turn out just as well as – and sometimes better than – kids from traditional families with two heterosexual parents. Findings have been remarkably similar, whether studies have focused on families with lesbian mothers, gay fathers, transgender parents, or single mothers by choice. Findings on families created by donations of eggs, sperm, or embryos, as well as by surrogacy, reflect the same pattern.

In studies of all these new forms of family, we, along with other research teams, have found that the quality of family relationships matters for children's welfare far more than the number, gender, gender identity, sexual orientation, or biological relatedness of the parents.

It has taken nearly 50 years of studies, many following children across decades, to establish the empirical evidence. And there has been plenty of heartache along the way, starting with lesbian mothers who lost custody of their children back in the 1970s. In the half century since then, public and expert fears about new forms of family have underpinned various legal barriers to parenthood, discriminatory practices, and widespread stigmatization.

More new forms of family coming

However, even though research on children's outcomes is clear, the story does not end there, for two reasons. First, the diversity of new family forms seems likely only to expand as science advances and people seek new paths to parenthood. Artificial wombs, eggs, and sperm are just over the horizon. At the University of Cambridge Centre for Family Research, we are already examining children's outcomes in co-parenting families in which couples are not romantically involved, children are parented by single fathers by choice, and transgender people give birth after they have transitioned.

These developments pose fresh challenges to what has long been seen as the norm for children to flourish. Let's hope people avoid repeating over-hasty judgments. We should await the evidence and be calmed by encouraging outcomes from other new forms of family.

Children are asking for change

Second, and perhaps more important, there is much more to say about children in these new forms of family, beyond simply logging their long-term outcomes. What is it like for

them to grow up in such families? We should listen to their voices, and hear their thoughts and feelings. To that end, our team has conducted many studies gathering children's stories.

Through our work, we have found that schools, parents, and the wider society still have much to learn about supporting children in non-traditional families through their experiences, which can be upsetting. The distress is not related to the type of family children have, but because of stigmatization, inadequate communication, and lack of understanding, mainly from those on the periphery of home.

So, for example, many children with LGBTQ parents have been stigmatized in school, by society, and sometimes by wider family. When we interviewed children of lesbian mothers born in the mid-1960s when they were young adults, almost half reported being teased or bullied as teenagers.

Stigmatization burdens children

'I wasn't allowed to go to my friend's house anymore,' said Anna. 'Her mum and dad forbade me from going anywhere near, and that hurt me because she had been my best friend for a long, long time. I lost that friend. And then, of course, there was a chain reaction. Everybody found out. They said, 'Don't go near her, she'll turn out like her mum.''

John was bullied when schoolmates found out about his lesbian mum. 'School was one big nightmare really, because I got picked on so much,' he explained. 'I had cigarettes stubbed out on the back of my neck, and high-heeled shoes thrown at me, and a bit of hair cut off, and my head chucked down the loo, and that sort of thing.'

Children have felt the need to clam up about their families because of widespread prejudice. Stacey explained: 'My brother and I knew some people in our school that had gay and lesbian parents and that did get bullied quite a lot, and that scared us from telling people. So, we never told anyone. It was hard keeping secrets.'

Effective school challenges to prejudice

Schools must create a positive, supportive environment for such children. It pays off. Carol, 14, highlighted helpful action by her school: 'Basically, they spread the word how it's not very good to say, "Oh this is so gay" or "that's so gay," even though it's used as a different meaning. They tell them that's wrong and why you shouldn't say that.' Mike, 17, recalled how a new English teacher, who was gay, made a difference: 'He has one of the Stonewall "Some People

Are Gay, Get Over It" posters in his classroom. Just seeing the poster in his room is really cool.' As part of our research project, the UK campaign for equality of LGBTQ people, Stonewall, published 10 recommendations from children on how schools can support them and their same-sex parents.

Children of transgender parents have been bullied and teased in similar ways, and inclusive attitudes by schools can help them. Wendy explained: 'I put my hand up and said, "I don't have a dad because my dad's transgender," and I got an award for it 'cos it was actually really brave of me to say.'

Tell children what's happening

Parents also should consider being more open about what is happening in their families. 'It would have helped if he had explained things a bit better,' said Henry, 18, reflecting on when his father transitioned to being a woman. 'It wasn't so much him wearing dresses, but more him being a bit manic and doing strange things.' Chris, 18, advised other children in a similar situation: 'Try to get them to communicate with you as much as possible because it's worse if things are happening and you don't know why.'

Children tend to accept, in a matter of fact way, their father's or mother's change of gender if it happened while they were little or a long time ago. 'Chloe's always been Chloe,' said Susanna, 14, who was a toddler when her father transitioned. 'I don't remember when it actually happened, so it's basically been for as long as I remember.'

Experiencing transition can worry them

But some children find it difficult when they experience a parent's transition. They can have fears of loss, which typically pass, but which can be very real during gender transition. Jade, who was six when her father transitioned, was upset about losing her dad: 'When she transitioned, I felt like there was a hole in my heart because I missed my dad and every time somebody talked about their dad, I got really upset.' But she grew more accepting. At age nine, Jade reflected: 'When she transitioned, it made her a lot happier 'cos, when she was a boy, she was really unhappy. Ever since she's transitioned, she's come home from work, hugged us, and been really happy. It's changed a lot since she transitioned.'

Another upset can be rejection of parents by their wider family, so children lose contact with some relatives. Theresa, whose father transitioned when she was six, explained: 'People on my mum's side of the family really struggle with it. Her parents and brothers, and basically everyone over there, cut us off. It made me sad and kind of angry because it's really no reason to be horrible.'

Children should not have to explain their families

Children may also feel responsible for explaining to the outside world issues such as gender transition. 'My problem,' explained Susanna, 'has been having to explain to other people constantly because no one really understands.' Josh reported: 'Sometimes, random people ask me questions and I have to explain to them. That gets tiring for me.'

Our research has highlighted issues for children born through assisted reproductive technologies, such as egg, sperm, and embryo donation, or surrogacy. Some children as young as two or three years might ask of a single mother by choice: 'Do I have a daddy? Where is he?' Some – but by no means all – especially as they get into their teens, are eager to fill a gap in knowledge about themselves by finding out more about their donor, surrogate, and any half-siblings born to the same donor or surrogate.

'It's important to me now . . . I'm always thinking about what she looks like,' explained Sarah, 14, who was born through egg donation. Alex, 14, conceived by sperm donation, said: 'I would like to know who he is . . . quite a lot . . . Recently a lot more than I used to.'

Tell children early about their origins

We have found that it is generally better to start talking to children early about how they were conceived and born. Children who find out later, as teenagers or adults, tend to feel more negatively about how they were conceived and in their relationships with their parents than children who have had the conversation about their beginnings early. Many parents hold off telling their children, fearing that the children will love them less. However, these fears are unfounded because children who are told early tend to be very accepting, often not particularly interested, and unshocked by learning more as they grow older.

The risks of not disclosing this information to children have grown with the advent of ancestry sites offering DNA tests, which can suddenly lead unsuspecting children to discover half-siblings and relatives of whom they had no inkling. Children may find their identities destabilized, and learning about their beginnings in this way can undermine their trust in their parents.

The story of new forms of family is largely good news, of children flourishing, much as we might expect them to do in traditional families, and sometimes doing even better. The composition of their family does not upset them. It is other factors, such as people's reactions to their family or the lack of information about their origins, that cause them distress. The solutions lie in better understanding, greater societal acceptance of diverse families, swift challenges to prejudice, and openness within families about where their much-wanted children came from.

October 2020

Happy Families?

Chapter 2

The importance of having a good relationship with your family

Families teach you to communicate

A family that communicates is a healthy family. Each member learns to communicate their opinions, thoughts and feelings. They're encouraged to share them and respect those of the other members in their family.

Communication is especially important if you're far away from home. You don't have to feel isolated and it pays to browse the different broadband and phone deals out there. Some of these packages include reduced rate international calls. Not everyone is aware of it, though, and sometimes fail to keep in touch with their families as a result.

Families offer safety

Enjoying a good relationship with your family can make you feel safe and protected. There's always someone in the world who will look out for you. You may have your faults, but they'll always have your back. When things go wrong, there's a sense of togetherness. You're all going through the experience, good or bad.

Families build trust

Since families go through the good times and the bad ones together, they build trust in each other. As a result of being in a healthy family, you learn not just to trust each other, but also others in society. And since the family is the basic unit for teaching children about relationships, you'll be able to form better bonds outside of the family.

Families teach responsibility

To get by in life, you have to be able to fulfil commitments and cope with responsibilities, such as paying the rent and bills on time and holding down a job. Not only that, you have to be a responsible citizen and respect the city in which you live. In a family, each member assumes certain responsibilities, from which the family as a whole benefits and becomes stronger. Family teaches the importance of responsibility, laying the foundations for us to grow up as responsible people.

Families teach you to deal with conflict

You're not always going to get on with every member of your family all the time. There will be conflict, but you'll learn to resolve it respectfully. No matter how you feel inside, you'll learn that violence and aggression aren't the way to deal with things. You'll see that dialogue is the way to address conflicts and to start finding solutions for other problems.

Having a good relationship with your family is crucial. We learn so much from them: how to trust, how to communicate, how to handle responsibility and more. If ever you move away from home, make sure you've built a solid relationship with your family, so you can navigate life knowing they're there for you, even if they can only be at the other end of the phone.

31 July 2020

www.lnreview.co.uk

How your family relationships influence you

Does my relationship with my parents affect my character? And can my relationship with my brother or sister affect who my friends are?

By Dr. Sunil Raheja

Family is very important; the relationships between us and our mother, father, sister or brother are the first relationships we learn to form in our lives. So it is not surprising that these relationships can have a significant impact on us later in life and even determine how well we form new relationships in the future.

We spoke to Dr Sunil Raheja, an experienced consultant psychiatrist based in London, to find out more about family dynamics and how they influence our behaviour later in life.

How does your family influence you and your behaviour?

Your family influences your behaviour in a tremendous way. We learn so much about how we interact with the world and ourselves. Family relationships cast long shadows, especially when we are young, and it goes very deep into our psyche. Young children are like sponges; they learn so much from their parents and/or caregivers and there are many ways it can affect them as they grow up:

* Physical health - Many studies have shown that positive relationships with relatives lead to more positive habits later in life, such as taking better care of yourself and making healthy food choices. In contrast, negative relationships that cause stress can lead to unhealthy eating habits and poor physical self-care.

* Mental health - A strong and positive family support system from a young age can lead to better mental health when we are adults. As children, we need to feel loved and supported, which can give us a sense of purpose in our lives as we grow up and enter adulthood. Without this, we humans tend to grow up vulnerable to developing mental health disorders.

* Emotional health - Having positive sibling relationships can teach us how to interact and build friendships with other children of different ages. It also teaches us how to share and builds empathy. However, problematic sibling relationships, such as rivalry or competition for a parent's love, can have a negative impact on us later in life.

Can your family influence your relationships with friends and colleagues?

As we get older, we begin to relate to people who remind us of certain members of our family because it brings up things from our past that we are not aware of. For example, if you had a bad relationship with your father, you may get angry with someone you meet who reminds you of him. However, it also works the other way around; you can build healthy relationships with people who remind you of a positive relationship you also had with your father.

What is a healthy family relationship?

A healthy family dynamic is one where all members feel loved, safe, and supported by each other; where all members of a family are able to feel comfortable with each other and your individual identity (your own and your place in the family) encourages you to grow and develop.

'All happy families are alike; each unhappy family is unhappy in its own way.' Leo Tolstoy

Every family functions differently, but parents and caregivers can help to foster this in their children by showing and teaching them love, care, positivity and respectful interaction.

How can you maintain a good relationship with your family?

A healthy family dynamic can be achieved by spending quality time together as a family, solving problems together and effectively communicating verbally and through actions how much you love one another.

It is important to remember that relationships are something organic and in a constant state of change. In order for parents to maintain a healthy relationship with their children, it is very important that they give them enough space to develop independently. Often parents make the mistake of treating their children younger than they actually are.

Individual space for children and especially teenagers is very important as it gives them time to do inner work, discover themselves and become more independent. It is a valuable growing space where they learn to discover what they want from life.

Unfortunately, some parents push their children to live out the dreams they once had for themselves; in other words, they live their lives through their child. Signs that you are doing this are that you are obsessing over your child's activities and/or forcing them to do things that don't seem to interest them. This can be very damaging to your child's self-identification.

'The greatest burden a child must bear is the unlived life of its parents.' Carl Jung

When might family therapy be needed?

Family therapy can be useful if there are problems that are becoming unsolvable and interfering with the daily lives of you and your family. Some outside help is then helpful.

Family therapy is not something you should shy away from; it can be an opportunity for all family members to develop and grow. Having someone from the outside commenting, speaking and pointing out patterns can help all members develop better self-awareness and a new perspective.

Each family has its own culture. Therapy can observe what is going on and make comments about the way members interact with each other. It can make you question what is 'normal' or acceptable behaviour.

Some problems that family therapy can help with are:

- Problems in communication
- Sibling rivalry
- Secrets and unresolved disputes
- Mental illness in the family
- Problems at school or work
- Behavioural problems
- Drug abuse or addiction
- A death in the family
- Financial problems

Family therapy creates a space where members can calmly and safely discuss their problems. It has great potential to be very healing and transformative.

23 June 2021

Nurturing dads raise emotionally intelligent kids – helping make society more respectful and equitable

An article from The Conversation.

By Kevin Shafer, Associate Professor of Sociology and Director of Canadian Studies, Brigham Young University

When my oldest son, now nearly 13, was born in July of 2008, I thought I could easily balance my career and my desire to be far more engaged at home than my father and his generation were. I was wrong.

Almost immediately, I noticed how social policies, schools and health care systems all make it difficult for dads to be highly involved and engaged at home. Contradictory expectations about work and family life abound.

As a fatherhood researcher with four kids of my own, I am convinced that fathers are transformative figures for children, families and communities.

But a man's mere presence, paycheck and willingness to punish misbehaving children is not nearly enough. Many of the benefits of fathering for children come from dads being nurturing, loving and engaged in all aspects of parenting.

When fathers are caregivers – when they provide emotional support and act affectionately toward their kids – the effects go well beyond growth, development, good health and solid grades. My research shows the benefits also include having children who value emotional intelligence, gender equality and healthy competition.

Nurturing versus stoic dads

Thinking about the broad impact fathers have, I analysed how fathering affects different social values – such as a belief in gender equality – in May 2021.

Surveying more than 2,500 American fathers 18 and older, I found that involved fathering has a long-lasting impact on the personal principles and cultural perspectives of children.

In my survey, the differences between the least nurturing and the most nurturing fathers are stark.

Surveyed fathers who reported that their own fathers were highly withdrawn tended to be hypercompetitive, emotionally stoic and unappreciative of women's contributions outside the home.

Fathers' attitudes and level of involvement of their dads

Fathers who did not have nurturing dads were more hypercompetitive, less emotionally open and less appreciative of gender equality.

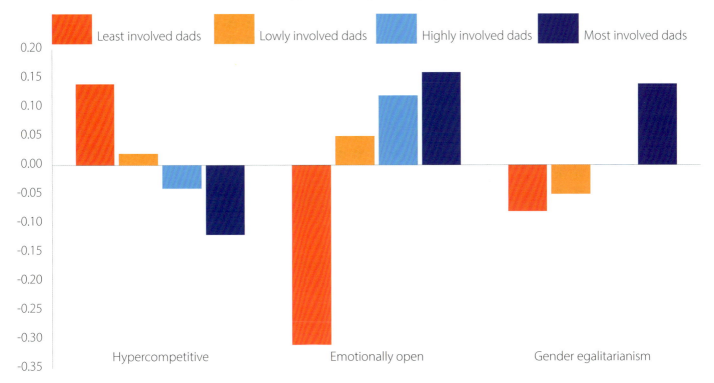

Source: Kevin Shafer, Brigham Young University

In contrast, surveyed fathers who said they had highly nurturing dads were much more likely to achieve their goals in a healthy manner, be more emotionally open and believe in equitable partnership.

How dads instil values

Several decades ago, many fathers were unwilling or unable to provide their children with emotional support or physical care. Instead, they focused on bread-winning, children's discipline and simply being present in the home.

These traditional norms left many contemporary fathers ill-equipped for modern parenthood. Contemporary social norms set broad expectations for fathers: rule enforcement and economically supporting the family while also providing for children's physical and emotional needs.

Broad paternal involvement with kids is important because dads have unique effects on kids. Children's values, beliefs, emotional expression and social development are strongly associated with fathering. Kids are better regulated emotionally, more resilient and more open-minded when their fathers are involved in their education and socialization.

Boys, for better and worse, often mirror the habits, interests and values of their own fathers.

My colleague Scott Easton and I found that how one's father behaves is especially powerful given that cultural, social and institutional norms about fatherhood are much weaker than they are for motherhood.

For example, mothers have traditionally been known for showing children affection and providing emotional support. Social expectations for these behaviors are not well defined among fathers. As a result, dads have a much larger impact on their sons' fathering behaviors than mums have on their daughters' mothering behaviors.

Positively, this means that a sizable portion of men replicate the best attributes of their own fathers – such as being loving and affectionate. Negatively, this means bad behaviors – such as extremely harsh discipline – are sometimes repeated across generations.

However, some men compensate for their own fathers' poor or nonexistent parenting by forming their own ideas and values about parenting.

Benefits for all

The findings from my survey build on decades of research on the benefits of positive fathering. And these advantages aren't just for children.

Mothers and other parenting partners are healthier and happier when fathers are highly engaged with their kids. Men who care for and support their kids benefit too – with improved self-image, life purpose and relationships. And communities gain increased trust and safety from the relationships built when fathers positively participate in their kids' activities, schooling and social networks.

Valuing supportive fathers

How can American society ensure that healthy competition, emotional openness and respect for women are widespread among future generations of men and fathers? Part of the answer is by valuing loving, supportive fathering.

That means more support for fathers in workplaces, public policy and institutions. Paid family leave, flexible work arrangements and integration of fathers into prenatal and postnatal care are all effective ways to encourage fathers to be more involved.

Many fathers increased their share of child care tasks during the COVID-19 pandemic. These shifts may become permanent, ultimately changing cultural values around parenting and gender roles.

Society also needs to provide clearer messaging to fathers about what does and does not work in parenting. For example, my colleagues and I have shown that men who believe they should be nurturing parents are more involved in their children's lives. Fathers who demonstrate healthy masculine traits like assertiveness and strong goal orientation also tend to be sensitive, engaged parents.

Thus, there are many routes to transformative fathering. And this is not simply behavior for biological fathers. Fatherhood is broadly defined, and people often look to nonbiological father figures like relatives, stepfathers, foster fathers and unrelated mentors.

All men who support and care for children have a critical role to play in instilling positive social values in future generations.

16 June 2021

The key to raising a happy family – and why it makes a difference

A new report has explored what can improve a child's chances of success and no matter who is part of the household, there's a theme...

By Peter Stanford

The occasions when our children sit down to eat round the kitchen table with me and my wife are getting fewer. But both my children are in their early 20s, have flown the nest and are busy getting on with independent lives, which is exactly as it should be.

That doesn't mean I don't occasionally mourn the empty chairs, but they still seem to want to come home often enough. And, when they do, it inevitably ends up with the family ritual of eating together, usually (but not inevitably) getting on harmoniously over dishes they associate with childhood (though, with one embracing veganism, it requires some adjustments to the recipes).

According to data published in an independent review of contemporary family life by Dame Rachel de Souza, the Children's Commissioner for England, families who eat together tend to be happier. So perhaps we have been doing something right these past two decades – though experience as a parent taught me long ago that the moment you start patting yourself on the back is also the moment when things start to go badly wrong.

Moreover, the margins between right and wrong in family matters can be narrow, as the report makes clear.

Among families who eat dinner together six days a week, 75 per cent profess themselves happy with life, as against a general level of 70 per cent among all families. I have a feeling that we only managed it four or five times some weeks when the kids were young and the sofa and the telly beckoned. Perhaps I shouldn't be as happy as I am.

A trivial point, but one that illustrates the difficulty of data-driven prescriptions that reveal a magic formula for family life. That is especially true at a time when, as Dame Rachel's report makes plain, families are more diverse than ever, with 23 per cent of children in this country living in lone-parent households (almost double the level of the rest of Europe) and 44 per cent who do not spend their entire childhood living with both biological parents.

What the report is keen to do, therefore, is focus on the family unit in all its manifestations, not just the mum, dad and 2.2 children nuclear model, but also those that mix in and rely on grandparents, aunts, uncles, godparents, neighbours and close friends. But it pulls no punches in arguing that having a stable family sees children flourish more than they would without it.

This is not a question of counting meals eaten at the same table, but rather of the cumulative 'protective' effect that an environment of love, support and togetherness delivers better than the alternatives. The family, Dame Rachel writes, is the 'most powerful foundation for the future', offering 'universal values' and 'provable protections'.

She quotes research evidence that children in stable families do better – in GCSEs, for example. And, if they get on with both their parents at 13, they will earn more (2 per cent more) by the time they are 25 than those who don't. 'This doesn't mean there is any blame for those who do not,' the Children's Commissioner insists, 'but it's a goal that we all want to achieve.'

Lone-parent households in Europe

Proportion of households headed by a single parent

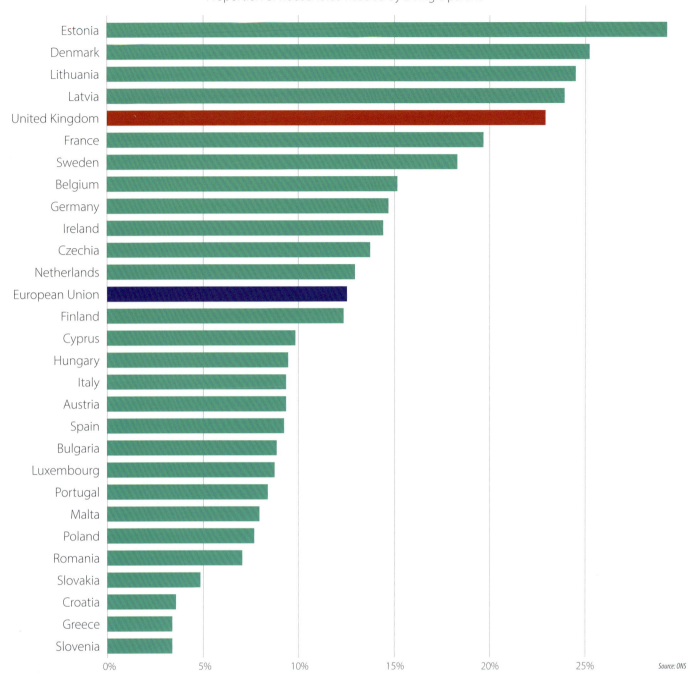

Source: ONS

Her emphasis is on promoting best practice. 'The word "family"- has been thrown around and politicised in recent years,' says Sarah Johnson, a writer on good parenting whose organisation, The Baby Experience, supports mums and dads going back to work after having a child to achieve a work-life balance in their fledgling family. 'It can be used in an exclusive way, to mean only the traditional nuclear family, but in my work I see many same-sex couples who are very good parents, intensely committed to becoming the sort of good, stable, sustaining family that Dame Rachel is championing.'

If the importance of family in growing the next generation is generally accepted, what specific measures does the report want to see introduced to encourage it to flourish?

It challenges the government to do more to help couples stay together and build the sort of families that produce the

desired outcome of successful, well-adjusted children who become successful, well-adjusted adults.

For more concrete proposals, rather frustratingly, we must wait for the second part of her report, due out in several months' time. But having laid out a vision of providing genuine, tailored support to sustain families, rather than 'faceless services', there are plenty of opinions on what is required.

'There is no such thing as a perfect family,' says eminent psychotherapist Julia Samuel, author of the current bestseller *Every Family Has A Story: How We Inherit Love and Loss*. She cautions against implementing the de Souza report on the basis that the family is a flawless institution.

'All families move between function and dysfunction, often because of the events that impact upon them. The current cost of living crisis is a good example. That safe, warm

kitchen table, with everyone gathered round, may seem a little less secure and even a bit more shouty when parents are struggling to make ends meet.'

However, that doesn't mean she disagrees with the thrust of the Children's Commissioner's findings. 'The alternative to the family is isolation and being alone, navigating life, or children learning to navigate life, without a close group around them. And that is much worse.'

In terms of specific measures that an incoming prime minister could introduce to bolster the family's place at the heart of our society, Cristina Odone from the Family Policy Unit at the Centre for Social Justice believes the first priority must be investing in early-years support. 'That means funding more health visitors and family hubs for those with small children, so that any issues are addressed early before they have grown into a crisis.'

Sarah Johnson concurs. 'There is just too little support at present for new parents – much less, for example, than in our near neighbours in Europe. Especially in the Netherlands, where health visitors are available for an extended period every day after a new baby is brought home.' This is when, she points out, marriages can start to fracture under the strain of life-changing events. 'We know from research that, for around a third of new parents, the arrival of children can be a pinch point in their partnership, where it can start to break down.'

Pressures placed by work on family life are also highlighted in the report, especially for fathers who want to play a fuller part in family life. During the Covid lockdown, the amount of time, on average, that dads spent with their children rose from 47 to 90 minutes a day. Now, it is back down to 56.

If modern working patterns mean that parents can no longer be there for every aspect of family life, Dame Rachel proposes a network of childcare facilities and playgroups. These would be run by hands-on neighbourhoods and communities with government support.

'Everyone in my field knows that it takes a village to raise a child who grows up reliable, resilient and robust,' says psychotherapist Julia Samuel. 'These are characteristics they can learn not just from their parents but by having different people in their everyday life, people who they know, who know them, and who they trust.'

That family kitchen table may need to become an extendable one.

1 September 2022

Why family mealtime is so important

By Laura Burgess

From the '50s to the early '70s, the average family rarely, if ever, ate out. It was normal to have all hands on deck when it came to preparing the family dinner and to sit down together to eat without any interruptions. This was decades before the arrival of what's now known as 'the digital dinner table' generation.

That's right; no tablets or smartphones, no sitting in front of the TV, no games consoles and certainly no internet. Nowadays, we are so easily distracted during our 'down time' in the evenings, and it's not just us as adults. More importantly, I'm talking about our little ones who, by the time they have come home from school, are sat in front of the TV, eyes glued to mobile and dinner on a tray.

Even without these distractions, we also have so much choice available to us on the high street that it's easy to pick up a readymade snack on the way home from school or to call into a fast food restaurant instead. Everything is so readily available and cheap. It was in the early '70s that food giants such as McDonald's opened their doors and now we are flooded by them.

The Mediterranean diet is often cited as one of the healthiest diets in the world but have we ever considered that it's not just the food itself (olive oil, fish and vegetables) that

impacts the longevity and quality of life? Part of it is down to the love and care that goes into the preparation. Then there's the time allocated for sitting down with loved ones (think immediate family, cousins and friends) to talk and eat, and talk some more. Mealtimes last for at least two hours and there is a real sense of community, whereas the average dinnertime in the UK is only 21 minutes.

Meanwhile, back in the UK, recent research from YouGov's Children's Omnibus that surveyed 1,789 children, found that one in three (34%) eat their evening meal in front of the TV, whilst around three in ten (29%) do the same for breakfast. Although the research found that eight in ten (82%) do eat dinner at the table, it also discovered that youngsters become less sociable with their meals as they get older by eating in their bedroom.

The traditional practice of families eating good food around the table together, as in places like the Mediterranean, can be enormously beneficial for children. So, whilst traditional manners used to be about teaching kids not to talk with their mouths full, keeping elbows off the table and staying seated until everyone else was finished, it's time to impart the new generation's rules of switching off technology and sitting down together for at least 45 minutes to an hour.

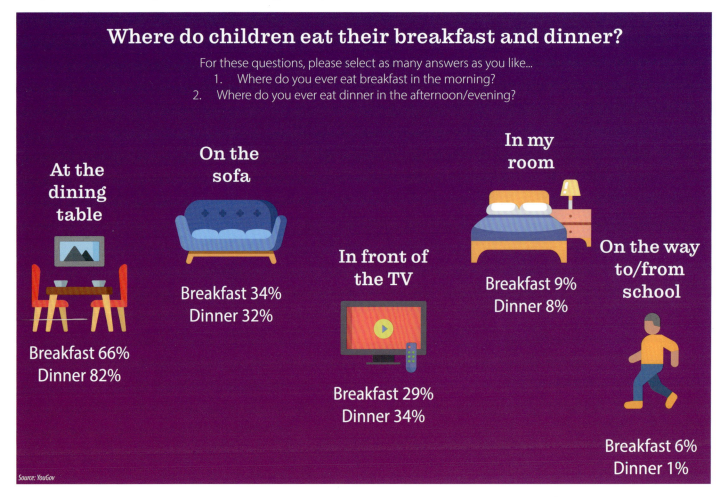

Where do children eat their breakfast and dinner?

For these questions, please select as many answers as you like...
1.   Where do you ever eat breakfast in the morning?
2.   Where do you ever eat dinner in the afternoon/evening?

At the dining table
Breakfast 66%
Dinner 82%

On the sofa
Breakfast 34%
Dinner 32%

In front of the TV
Breakfast 29%
Dinner 34%

In my room
Breakfast 9%
Dinner 8%

On the way to/from school
Breakfast 6%
Dinner 1%

Source: YouGov

Here are the reasons why.

1. Family dinners lead to better relationships

Eating together helps build a closer relationship with your children and is an opportunity for everyone in the family to learn more about each other. For younger children, dinnertime conversation can boost vocabulary. Regular mealtimes mean you can connect and find out what's going on at school, for example. Family dinners also lower the high-risk teenage behaviours that parents fear, such as smoking, binge drinking and eating disorders. Of course, sitting in stony silence or scolding kids at the table won't lead to positive benefits but sharing a positive experience, joke or story are small muments that lead to building stronger connections.

2. Healthier food choices are made

Eating together as a family is associated with healthy dietary and nutritious patterns. Children are more likely to consume more vegetables and fruits and less fizzy drinks and fried foods, which means that with the correct eating habits in place, they are less likely to be overweight. Meals that are prepared at home are usually a lot healthier than meals eaten whilst dining out and it's a great way to save money. It's also an opportunity to expand your taste buds and have fun in the kitchen by making healthy versions of popular foods, such as pizza, by getting your kids involved too.

3. Improvement in academic performance

Studies have proven that family dinners significantly improve school grades. Teenagers who eat with their family four or more times a week also have higher academic performance. Researchers found that teens who have fewer than three family dinners in a typical week are more than twice as likely to do poorly in school. Talk around the dinner table can be encouraging, with children believing that their parents are proud of them.

4. Stronger mental health

Teenagers that eat with their parents regularly are more likely to be emotionally strong and have better mental health. Children are more likely to have good manners and better communication skills. It's also a chance for your child to practise their social skills. It's the perfect opportunity to build self-esteem as listening to your child shows that you value and respect who they are, what they do and how important they are to you.

5. Eating at home saves money

It's cheaper to cook meals at home than to dine out. Home cooked meals cost two to four times less than those purchased in a restaurant. Planning a menu saves money so that when you go food shopping you will know exactly what to purchase. It's a good idea to sit your family down and come up with a list of ten foods that everyone loves. You can keep the list to hand and find ways to mix and match so you don't have to overspend. Frozen fruit and vegetables are great for making healthy family dinners on a budget.

These days, eating meals in front of the TV instead of around the table has become the social norm but the benefits suggest that it's time to revert to traditional mealtimes. Eating together promotes more sensible eating habits, good mental wellbeing and gets you and your family into a loving routine that, hopefully, your children will take with them when they fly the nest and will one day pass onto their own kids.

24 April 2019

Yes, more and more young adults are living with their parents – but is that necessarily bad?

An article from The Conversation.

By Jeffrey Arnett, Senior Research Scholar, Department of Psychology, Clark University

When the Pew Research Center reported in 2020 that the proportion of 18-to-29-year-old Americans who live with their parents has increased during the COVID-19 pandemic, perhaps you saw some of the breathless headlines hyping how it's higher than at any time since the Great Depression.

From my perspective, the real story here is less alarming than you might think. And it's actually quite a bit more interesting than the sound bite summary.

For 30 years I've been studying 18-to-29-year-olds, an age group I call 'emerging adults' to describe their in-between status as no longer adolescents, but not fully adult.

Even 30 years ago, adulthood – typically marked by a stable job, a long-term partnership and financial independence – was coming later than it had in the past.

Yes, a lot of emerging adults are now living with their parents. But this is part of a larger, longer trend, with the percentage going up only modestly since COVID-19 hit. Furthermore, having grown kids still at home is not likely to do you, or them, any permanent harm. In fact, until very recently, it's been the way adults have typically lived throughout history. Even now, it's a common practice in most of the world.

Staying home is not new or unusual

Drawing on the federal government's monthly Current Population Survey, the Pew Report showed that 52% of 18-to-29-year-olds are currently living with their parents, up from 47% in February. The increase was mostly among the younger emerging adults – ages 18 to 24 – and was primarily due to their coming home from colleges that shut down or to their having lost their jobs.

Although 52% is the highest percentage in over a century, this number has, in fact, been rising steadily since hitting a low of 29% in 1960. The main reason for the rise is that more and more young people continued their education into their 20s as the economy shifted from manufacturing to information and technology. When they're enrolled in school, most don't make enough money to live independently.

Before 1900 in the United States, it was typical for young

people to live at home until they married in their mid-20s, and there was nothing shameful about it. They usually started working by their early teens – it was rare then for kids to get even a high school education – and their families relied upon the extra income. Virginity for young women was highly prized, so it was moving out before marriage that was scandalous, not staying home where they could be shielded from young men.

In most of the world today, it is still typical for emerging adults to stay home until at least their late 20s. In countries where collectivism is more highly valued than individualism – in places as diverse as Italy, Japan and Mexico – parents mostly prefer to have their emerging adults stay home until marriage. In fact, even after marriage it remains a common cultural tradition for a young man to bring his wife into his parents' household rather than move out.

Until the modern pension system arose about a century ago, aging parents were highly vulnerable and needed their adult children and daughters-in-law to care for them in their later years. This tradition persists in many countries, including the two most populous countries in the world, India and China.

In today's individualistic U.S., we mostly expect our kids to hit the road by age 18 or 19 so they can learn to be independent and self-sufficient. If they don't, we may worry that there is something wrong with them.

You'll miss them when they're gone

Because I've been researching emerging adults for a long time, I've been doing a lot of television, radio and print interviews since the Pew report was released.

Always, the premise seems to be the same: Isn't this awful?

I would readily agree that it's awful to have your education derailed or to lose your job because of the pandemic. But it's not awful to live with your parents during emerging adulthood. Like most of the rest of family life, it's a mixed bag: It's a pain in some ways, and rewarding in others.

In a national survey of 18-to-29-year-olds I directed before the pandemic, 76% of them agreed that they get along better with their parents now than they did in adolescence, but almost the same majority – 74% – agreed, 'I would prefer to live independently of my parents, even if it means living on a tight budget.'

Parents express similar ambivalence. In a separate national survey I directed, 61% of parents who had an 18-to-29-year-old living at home were 'mostly positive' about that living arrangement, and about the same percentage agreed that living together resulted in greater emotional closeness and companionship with their emerging adults. On the other hand, 40% of the parents agreed that having their emerging adults at home meant worrying about them more, and about

25% said it resulted in more conflict and more disruption to their daily lives.

As much as most parents enjoy having their emerging adults around, they tend to be ready to move on to the next stage of their lives when their youngest kid reaches their 20s. They have plans they've been delaying for a long time – to travel, to take up new forms of recreation and perhaps to retire or change jobs.

Those who are married often view this new phase as a time to get to know their spouse again – or as a time to admit their marriage has run its course. Those who are divorced or widowed can now have an overnight guest without worrying about scrutiny from their adult child at the breakfast table the next morning.

My wife, Lene, and I have direct experience to draw on with our 20-year-old twins, who came home in March after their colleges closed, an experience shared with millions of students nationwide. I'll admit we were enjoying our time as a couple before they moved back in, but nevertheless it was a delight having them unexpectedly return, as they are full of love and add so much liveliness to the dinner table.

Now the fall semester has started and our daughter, Paris, is still home taking her courses via Zoom, whereas our son, Miles, has returned to college. We're savouring these months with Paris. She has a great sense of humour and makes an excellent Korean tofu rice bowl. And we all know it won't last.

That's something worth remembering for all of us during these strange times, especially for parents and emerging adults who find themselves sharing living quarters again. It won't last.

You could see this unexpected change as awful, as a royal pain and daily stress. Or you could see it as one more chance to get to know each other as adults, before the emerging adult sails once again over the horizon, this time never to return.

13 October 2020

One in twelve parents say they regret having children

But many parents, and younger ones in particular, wish they'd had more kids.

By Eir Nolsoe

Online forums such as Mumsnet, Reddit and Quora are full of threads with guilt-ridden parents who desperately ask if anyone else regrets having children too.

YouGov data shows that while the vast majority of parents (83%) insist they've never felt this way, a small number admit to it. One in twelve parents (8%) say they regret having children, while another 6% have previously had regrets but don't now.

While there's no difference between mothers and fathers, younger parents aged 25 to 34 are the most likely to feel regretful, with one in five either rueing their choice (13%) or having done so (9%).

Those aged 55+, for most of whom tantrum-throwing toddlers and sleep deprivation are a fading memory, are the least woeful. Only one in ten are unhappy with their decision to have children (6%) or have questioned it in the past (4%).

One in twelve parents regret having children

To what extent, if at all, do you regret having children? Have you ever regretted having children, and if so, to what extent? % of 1,206 parents

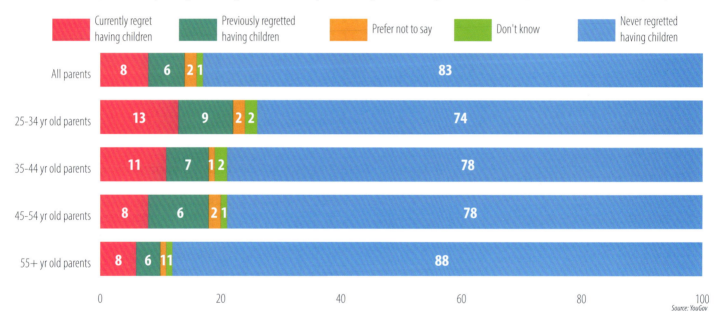

Source: YouGov

One in twelve parents regret having children

To what extent, if at all, do you regret having children? % of 1,249 British parents

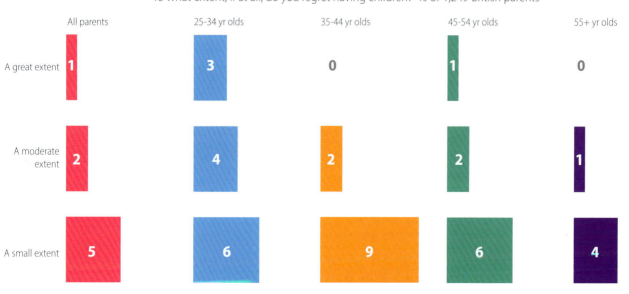

Source: YouGov

Younger parents are more likely to wish they'd had more children

Overall, if you could turn back time, would you... % of 1,017 British parents

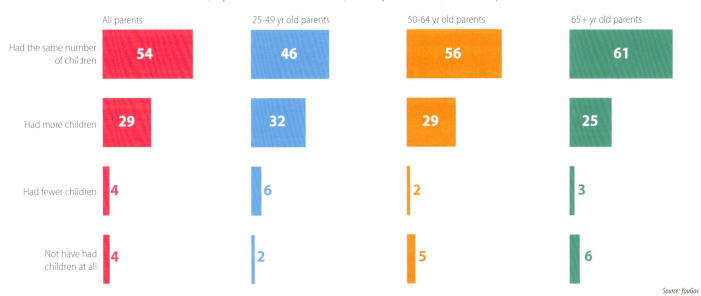

	All parents	25-49 yr old parents	50-64 yr old parents	65+ yr old parents
Had the same number of children	54	46	56	61
Had more children	29	32	29	25
Had fewer children	4	6	2	3
Not have had children at all	4	2	5	6

Source: YouGov

Mothers are more likely than fathers to say they wish they'd had more children

Overall, if you could turn back time, would you... % of 1,017 British parents

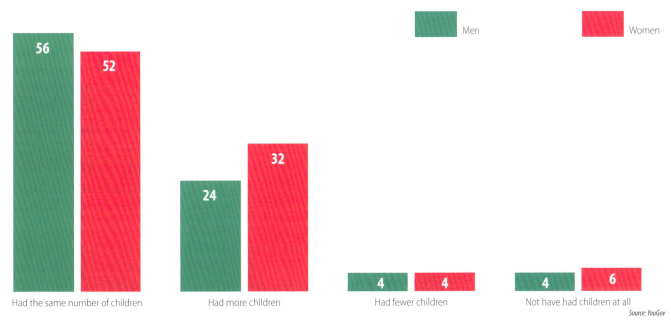

Men   Women

	Men	Women
Had the same number of children	56	52
Had more children	24	32
Had fewer children	4	4
Not have had children at all	4	6

Source: YouGov

Among the 8% of parents who still regret having kids, 5% say it's to a small extent, while for 2% it's to a moderate degree, and for 1% to a large extent.

The pattern is fairly similar among mothers and fathers who have previously been unhappy with parenthood, with 5% insisting their regrets were minor, and 1% saying they regretted it to a moderate degree.

Three in ten parents wish they'd had more children

While some 8% of parents currently feel regretful about their offspring, a separate survey shows that only half as many (4%) say they would not have had children if they could do it all again. A similar figure say they would have had fewer kids (4%). It's much more common for people to wish they'd had more children, at 29%. The majority (54%) would have the same number if given the option again.

A third of younger parents aged 25 to 49 (32%) wish they'd had more children, while parents in the oldest age group, 65+, are the least likely to say so at 25%. The UK's fertility rate is much lower today than in the 1960s and 70s, meaning younger Britons tend to have fewer children than their parents' generation.

In this instance there is also a difference between the genders, with a third of mothers (32%) wishing they'd had more children, compared with one in four fathers (24%).

24 June 2021

Help, my parents are getting divorced!

Parents getting divorced can be a traumatic and harrowing experience for people of any age, but it can be especially hard on teenagers. You're already trying to handle changes to your body, yo-yo emotions, and all the challenges that come with being a teenager – now you have all the stresses and upset that come with your parents getting divorced to deal with, too.

Dealing with divorce

There may be arguments happening at home or tensions running throughout the family which lead to you feeling upset, frustrated or even angry. It's perfectly normal to have a range of feelings about the situation but the main thing to always remember is that people split for many reasons, but **it is never your fault.**

Dealing with divorce can be incredibly stressful for everyone in the family. Each person in your family may handle their emotions differently but one thing you can all do to reduce frictions and upset is to communicate:

- Talk to your family about how you're feeling. Share your worries and concerns to get the support you need during this difficult time.

- Listen to your family members as they have listened to you and try to support them in any way you can. A simple hug, for example, can go a long way to making a younger sibling feel better.

- Ask questions. You probably have a lot of questions around the separation and are unsure of what is going to happen next. Some things might be sad to hear, but it can reduce your levels of anxiety when you have more clarity about the situation.

- If you don't feel able to speak up, or would prefer not to, write it down in a letter. Sometimes it can be easier to communicate the things we want to say by putting pen to paper.

It takes time

It's a cliché but it's true that this situation can get better in time. It can feel very turbulent in the beginning, especially when feelings are raw. There are a lot of complicated feelings and relationships involved when parents are getting divorced and it will take time for everyone involved to deal with their individual experiences.

It might also take time for the practical aspects of separation to take place, such as a parent moving out and into a new place, or for custody arrangements to be put in place. These situations are unlikely to be fixed overnight and it's perfectly normal to feel frustrated, but things can settle eventually.

When things get messy...

Sometimes, divorces can get messy and complicated. Very often, children can feel stuck in the middle, torn between the two people they love most in the world. This can lead to feelings of stress, pressure, and even guilt, as you try to strike the unfair balance of keeping both parents happy.

Talk to your parents about how the situation is making you feel or ask another family member to speak on your behalf. Being honest is the best way to let your parents know how their behaviour is affecting you.

Getting support

You and your family may need further support in dealing with divorce. Your doctor may be able to put you in touch with a therapist or you can talk to your school counsellor if one is available to you.

The above information is reprinted with kind permission from Hidden Strength.
© 2023 Hidden Strength

www.hiddenstrength.com

I feel torn between my parents

Are you stuck in the middle of arguing parents or in the midst of a family separation? We're here to help.

Arguments and break-ups can make you feel torn. You might be feeling pressure to 'choose a side' or to favour one parent over the other. It can cause a lot of anxiety and stress if your parents' actions are making you feel like a miserable piggy-in-the-middle, but you shouldn't have to suffer in silence.

Speak up

Try to talk to your parents about how their behaviour is making you feel. You can talk to them together or approach them separately if things are just too tense and strained.

If you feel too scared to speak to them directly – perhaps because you're worried it will start another argument or you're frightened to upset them – you could talk to another family member or a family friend and ask them to discuss your feelings with your parents on your behalf.

Be honest

Try to be as honest as you can when you explain how upsetting you find the situation. Be upfront and clear about your feelings, even if you're worried about upsetting one or both parents. Remember that arguments and breakups happen for all sorts of reasons, but it is never your fault.

Choosing your mument

If your parents are arguing a lot, it can be difficult to find the right time to raise the subject. Try to find a mument when things are calm as it can be extremely difficult to talk to someone who is angry or upset. You can make a note of your feelings or the incidents that are making you feel upset to help you communicate your thoughts more clearly.

Sibling support

It's a good idea to check in with siblings to see how they're coping with the situation. They might also be feeling the same as you and need a little support. Having the support of someone who is going through the exact same experience as you can be a great comfort.

It might be the case that your sibling has different views to you. While you might not agree with their thoughts it's important to understand that, ultimately, that's their choice. You can still find ways to have a relationship, even if you disagree with their decisions.

Getting more help

Sadly, communication sometimes completely breaks down between two people and nothing we say or do can change the situation. If the arguments continue or worsen, or you feel increasingly sad and stressed, you can reach out for more help. You can talk to a family member, family friend, your teacher, or a helpline to get support.

The above information is reprinted with kind permission from Hidden Strength.
© 2023 Hidden Strength

www.hiddenstrength.com

Adele's album is going to hit children of divorce hard – here's why

As the singer releases her long-awaited fourth album, Olivia Petter examines what it might mean to people from broken homes.

It happened when I was four. 'Oh that's so good,' said an old school friend, when I revealed the age I was when my parents had split up. 'At least you were young; I bet you barely even think about it now.' For a long time, I thought that was true.

Like everyone, I've been through my fair share of life's hurdles. But my parents' divorce never felt like one of them. I was so young when it happened; I've never known anything different, so there were no major complications. It's not like it's a rare thing to experience, either. Data from the Office of National Statistics states that the estimated divorce rate in the UK is 42 per cent, which means that over one in three marriages will end in divorce, leaving hundreds and thousands of children growing up in broken homes.

The commonality of it all is just one of the reasons why children of divorce, such as myself, rarely consider the implications. But that might be about to change. Today, 19 November, Adele has released her fourth studio album, 30 – and, as has been well publicised, it's about 'divorce, babe'.

In 2019, the 33-year-old singer split from her husband, Simon Konecki, after less than a year of marriage. Adele has said that she hopes the album will offer some form of catharsis to Angelo, the nine-year-old son she shares with Konecki.

'I just felt like I wanted to explain to him, through this record, when he's in his twenties or thirties, who I am and why I voluntarily chose to dismantle his entire life in the pursuit of my own happiness,' she told British Vogue. 'It made him really unhappy sometimes. And that's a real wound for me that I don't know if I'll ever be able to heal.'

It's a wound that Adele examines deeply. In 'Easy On Me', the only single that was dropped prior to the album's release, lyrics like 'You can't deny how hard I have tried, I changed who I was to put you both first' viscerally capture the pain that characterised the singer's decision to end her marriage. Such words started having an effect on fans from broken homes before the full album was even released.

'Realising in less than a week Adele's album comes out and I'll finally have to emotionally deal with my parents' divorce hearing Adele,' tweeted one person. 'No one talk to me when Adele's album comes out because it's about her explaining the divorce to her [nine]-year-old son and my VERY unresolved childhood trauma from my parents' separation and broken up family is going to absolutely thrive and ruin me in the process,' added another.

Here's the thing: divorce is an obvious catastrophe for everyone involved. But, as adults, we tend to focus on the experiences of people we know getting divorced rather than acknowledge the long-lasting impact on those who have grown up with separated parents. There are numerous reasons for this: namely that we're more likely to witness the trauma of divorce if someone we know is going through one. But there's also something to be said about how normalised divorce has become in our society to the point where, if it happened to your parents, it's spoken about with a flippancy akin to conversations about the weather.

This seems strange when you consider how much research has highlighted the consequences of coming from a broken home. Sure, some studies have found

> **If your parents got divorced, it's spoken about with a flippancy akin to conversations about the weather**

that children of divorce mature faster and become more independent. Others, however, have suggested that children of divorce are more likely to suffer from mental health issues, behavioural problems, and drug and alcohol dependencies.

What's more, is that children of divorce might be more likely to encounter problems in their own romantic relationships. 'Children of divorce can struggle in adult life with a fear of abandonment and trust issues with their partner,' says Jayne Hale, relationships counsellor at the charity Relate. 'Also, depending on how they experienced their parents communicating with each other, before and after the divorce, they may struggle with communication on an emotional level with their own partner later on.' They might also have difficulty being vulnerable with others, adds Hale, and struggle with low self-esteem.

There are obvious ways that having divorced parents has impacted on me: panic attacks whenever I heard them arguing, insomnia when my father remarried, and an overriding sense of displacement whenever one of them moved house. But these aren't things that are readily talked about or considered when it comes to understanding the experiences of children of divorce.

Instead it's having trouble settling down, being plagued by a fear of commitment, or having 'daddy issues' – a sexist remark attributed to any woman (never a man) whose father walked out on them.

Of course, some of these may ring true, but for me, the experiences I've found the most difficult are the ones I would have never linked to the divorce. Things that have only recently come to light – thank you, therapy – like a perpetual feeling of needing to belong, and a propensity to isolate myself from others when I need them the most. Then

there's the deeply rooted fear of getting divorced myself, a feeling that can be utterly paralysing when it comes to forming and ending romantic relationships.

This is something Adele, whose father walked out when she was two, has even alluded to herself. 'It made me really sad,' she told Rolling Stone of the realisation that her marriage was over. 'Then having so many people that I don't know know that I didn't make that work … it f***ing devastated me. I was embarrassed.'

Perhaps given how common divorce is, it's only natural that we'd normalise it. But to do so to the extent whereby we also normalise the trauma that results from it is a problem, particularly if you're experiencing that trauma unknowingly, as I was for many years. I'm not saying everything is better now I know where my issues stem from, but it's certainly reassuring – and makes them easier to work through.

I suspect today will be an emotional day for me and many others. Listening to the experiences of Adele and the messages she wants to send to Angelo will be gut-wrenching, and probably make me long for similar clarity from my own parents. But, knowing the success of an Adele album, it will also offer some hope that these important conversations are finally being started on a global scale. And as a result, children of divorce might feel a little less alone, even if just for the day.

17 November 2021

Family rifts affect millions – research shows possible paths from estrangement toward reconciliation

An article from The Conversation.

By Karl Pillemer, Hazel E. Reed Human Development Professor and Professor of Gerontology in Medicine, Cornell University

Family relationships are on many people's minds during the holiday season as sounds and images of happy family celebrations dominate the media. Anyone whose experiences don't live up to the holiday hype may find this difficult or disappointing, but those feelings may be felt even more acutely among those involved in family rifts.

I have done a significant amount of research on ambivalence and conflict in families, which led to a five-year study of family estrangements.

At the outset, I was surprised at how little evidence-based guidance exists on the frequency, causes and consequences of family estrangement, or how those involved cope with the stress of family rifts. There are few studies published in academic journals on the topic, as well as limited clinical literature. I sought to fill these gaps through a series of interrelated studies and have presented and described my findings in my 2020 book 'Fault Lines: Fractured Families and How to Mend Them.'

My findings suggest that estrangement is widespread and that there are several common pathways people take on the way to a family rift. Also, people who decide to try to close such a rift have discovered a number of different routes for getting to reconciliation.

Anyone can experience a family rift

To get an idea of how much estrangement is going on, in 2019 I conducted a national survey that asked the question: 'Do you have any family members (i.e., parents, grandparents, siblings, children, uncles, aunts, cousins or other relatives) from whom you are currently estranged, meaning you have no contact with the family member at the present time?'

The survey involved a nationally representative sample of 1,340 Americans aged 18 and older whose demographics closely mirrored the United States population.

The data from this survey revealed no statistically significant differences in estrangement according to a number of factors, including race, marital status, gender, educational level and region where the respondent lived. This finding suggests that estrangement is relatively evenly distributed in the population.

Over a quarter of the respondents – 27% – reported a current estrangement. Most had a rift with an immediate family member: 24% were estranged from a parent, 14% from a child and 30% from siblings. The remainder were estranged from other relatives.

There have yet to be any longitudinal studies on family rifts – studies that repeatedly survey participants with the same questions over time. So we do not know if estrangement is increasing or decreasing.

The sheer numbers, however, are striking. Extrapolating the national survey responses to the entire U.S. adult population suggests that around 68 million people have at least one current estrangement.

Pathways to estrangement

Between 2016 and 2020 my research team conducted 270 in-depth interviews with individuals who experienced estrangements, around 100 of whom had reconciled.

The findings of this study, which

are included in my book, reveal that there are multiple 'pathways' to estrangement: diverse trajectories toward family rifts that unfold across people's lives.

- **The long arm of the past.** The groundwork for a family estrangement can be established early in life, through disruptions and difficulties that occur while growing up. Harsh parenting, emotional or physical abuse or neglect, parental favouritism and sibling conflict can impair relationships decades into the future.

- **The legacy of divorce.** One frequent estrangement scenario involves the long-term effects of divorce in the lives of adult children. Loss of contact with one parent, or hostility between the former partners, can weaken parent-child bonds.

- **The problematic in-law.** In-law relations can be challenging under ordinary circumstances. But when the struggles between family of origin and family of marriage become intolerable, they can reach a breaking point.

- **Money and inheritance.** Conflicts over wills, inheritance and financial issues are a major source of family rifts.

- **Values and lifestyle differences.** Disapproval of a relative's core values can turn into outright rejection.

- **Unmet expectations.** Estrangement can result when relatives violate norms for what others believe is proper behaviour.

What about reconciliation?

This study was the first in the field to focus intensively on individuals who had successfully reconciled after years or decades of estrangement.

By carefully analysing their detailed accounts, my research team identified a number of strategies and approaches that worked for them:

- **Focus on the present.** Many interviewees reported that the history of the estranged relationship was inseparably interwoven with present circumstances. In some family rifts, the past almost entirely overwhelmed the present moment. As a result, many people interpreted relatives' present actions as signs or symptoms of underlying, decades-old pathologies. Nearly all who successfully reconciled reported that one key step was giving up attempts to force their interpretation of past events on the other person. They abandoned efforts to process the past and instead focused on the relationship's present and future.

- **Revise expectations.** Often respondents said that family values held them back from reconciling, because the other person had violated their standards for proper family life. Reconciliation involved modifying or dropping past expectations and abandoning the urge to force the relative to change.

- **Create clear boundaries.** Interviewees reported that making the terms of the reconciliation as unambiguous as possible was key to moving beyond old grievances and patterns of behaviour. Even people who had severed ties because of intolerable behaviours were able to create clear, specific, take-it-or-leave-it conditions for one final try to repair the relationship.

Whether or not to reconcile

Whether to attempt a reconciliation is a complicated decision. Some family situations involve damaging behaviour, a history of abuse or currently dangerous individuals. People experiencing these extreme situations may find that cutting off contact is the only solution, and a critical one for their safety and psychological well-being.

Many interviewees in challenging situations like these reported that working with a counselling professional helped them answer the question, 'Am I ready to reconcile?' In some cases, the answer was 'no.'

One positive finding of my research is that those who reconciled their rift found it to be an engine for personal growth. Reengaging with the family – after careful consideration and preparation – was almost never regretted.

However, it was a highly individual decision and not for everyone.

A need for knowledge

There are still gaps to fill in the basic research on how and why family rifts and reconciliations occur. Further, there is no evidence-based therapy or treatment for individuals coping with or trying to resolve estrangements. Therefore, intervention research is critically needed.

Expanding research and clinical insight on this widespread problem may help pave the way to solutions that will help not just at the holidays, but over the course of the entire year.

20 December 2021

Surviving siblings

Do you always get on well with your siblings? Love them or hate them we all sometimes have fallings out with our loved ones. Here are some tips on how to deal with some common issues.

They keep copying me!

Your sibling is copying (or 'borrowing') your clothes, belongings, music, etc.

While this can be extremely annoying, you need to remember that by stealing your style, they are actually showing you how much they respect you and your choices. They look upon you as a role-model and instead of losing it with them, try to help them to discover their own style. You do need to make it clear that they need to ask you before taking your stuff, but don't be too angry with them, after all imitation is the sincerest form of flattery!

Once they find their own style then they usually stop copying you. Sit down with them and tell them how it makes you feel as they may not realise how it's affecting you.

The green-eyed monster

You are jealous of your sibling, everything they do is better than you and you feel second-best.

Jealousy can be a difficult issue to overcome, and it can feel like our siblings are being treated differently, or that they have better presents than us at Christmas, or that they are cleverer than you.

Sometimes, parents and teachers make the feelings of jealousy worse with comments like 'why can't you be more like your sister/brother?'.

If you feel like this then you should speak to your parents or carers for reassurance. You will find that they do love you and your siblings equally.

Of course, our siblings may be better than us in a certain subject at school, but then we will be better at a different subject. The solution is not to compare yourself to them. You are an individual. Remember to focus on the things that you are good at, try to boost your self-esteem, as low self-esteem may be the root of your jealousy.

We keep arguing

You're always bickering with your siblings.

Unfortunately, not everyone gets on well with their siblings. Just because you are related to someone it doesn't mean you have to best of friends, but it does make life easier to keep the bickering to a minimum! Compromise is the key here, as no one ever really wins an argument. Try to stay calm, as a calm, considered approach will help you to get your point across rather than screaming and shouting at them. You could also ask to have a family meeting to work though any difficulties you may have with your sibling. Having your parents'/carers' point of view may help to resolve the matter and help to see if one or both of you are being unreasonable.

Having a sibling can be great, and you may find that as you both grow older you get along much better than you did as kids. Try to build a positive relationship with them as you only get one chance to do so.

Write

Imagine you have a problem with one of your siblings. Write a letter to an agony aunt/uncle describing the issue and then write a response which offers guidance on how to deal with the problem.

Create

Write your own guide on how to deal with your siblings. Either make a leaflet or poster on a 'Sibling Survival Guide'.

Arguing with the people you love? How to have a healthy family dispute

An article from The Conversation.

THE CONVERSATION

By Jessica Robles, Lecturer in Social Psychology, Loughborough University

Unlike Britain's royal family, most of us don't have the option to move to another country when we don't see eye to eye. But most of us have likely experienced disagreements with loved ones.

Conversations are designed to do things – to start some action, and complete it – whether it's a service transaction, an invitation to coffee or reassurance on a bad day. Our uniquely complex communicative system has evolved to help us get things done in the social world.

Arguments are part of this complex system. They can be unavoidable, necessary or even productive. But they can also be difficult.

It can be hard to know what to do when tensions are high and harsh words are flying, particularly when it involves someone you're close to. But research on how disputes unfold – and conversation more generally – offers some ideas about the best way to handle one.

What is a dispute?

There are many words for disagreeing, and there are plenty of academic theories describing what disputes are and why they happen. But arguments are not abstract models. They're lived in, breathed in, sweated in and talked (or sometimes shouted) into being.

Research focusing on how disputes actually happen shows they're characterised by three types of features. First are the vocal features, which include talking in a higher pitch, louder and faster. Then, there are embodied features such as aggressive gestures and avoidant stances, such as turning away from someone. Finally, there are interactional features such as talking over each other, not listening or metatalk – comments about the conversation as it's happening.

Displays of emotion such as displeasure or anger, are also common. Participants might accuse each other of emotions or label their own emotions.

Disputes happen for several reasons. What each person is doing can vary, from complaints and accusations to demands, threats or resistance.

They can be about many things – familial obligations, what to have for dinner, politics or how to plan a holiday. Luckily, disputes share elements with each other and with conversation generally – so you don't have to invent new strategies every time you're caught in one.

Affiliation and alignment

When bickering with a friend or family member, there are ways to make them feel like you're still on their side even if you disagree. If you can keep these in mind, and use them at the right time, you might stop your dispute from escalating into something harder to mend.

The first thing is affiliation, which means support for the other person or their view of things.

Affiliation involves phrasing what you say so it's best understood and easier to respond to. For example, saying 'you've been to France before, right?' invites someone to share their experience – partly by including the tag 'right' at the end, which at least requires a confirmation.

It can also involve categorisation, the way we talk about or treat others as certain types or group members. For example, if you reduce the other person to a stereotype through labelling – by saying something like 'girls always say stuff like that' or 'OK, boomer' – you risk provoking a response to the insult, not to the action in which that insult was embedded.

The second thing we expect from any conversation is alignment – cooperating with the direction of the conversation, such as accepting or denying a request. The opposite, disalignment, might occur when a request is ignored.

Alignment has more to do with the sequence of the conversation, how the dispute unfolds over time. Asking for clarification – a practice known as repair – or claiming a misunderstanding can treat problems as fixable errors rather than moral failings or attacks. Humour can diffuse conflict escalation.

How to have a healthy dispute

In the course of a dispute, you need to think about when to bring these tactics out. They're more likely to yield better outcomes earlier in the dispute. By the time it's escalated, your responses may be viewed through the prism of the dispute and any offensiveness you've already displayed toward each other. In cases like this, teasing can come across as contempt, for example, and claims to misunderstand as bad-faith mockery.

It can feel like disputes take on a life of their own – as if the conversation uses us rather than we use it – and this is partly because conversation can seemingly take us along for the ride (consider the difficulty of turning down invitations). We invest our identities into conversations so disputes can seem to threaten us and what we stand for morally.

This may be starker with family, whose opinions of us often matter more than friends or colleagues, for example. It's always worth stopping to reflect on what a dispute is really for, whether what you're saying lines up with your goals and whether taking a stand is worth it.

23 April 2021

www.theconversation.com

Useful Websites

www.childandfamilyblog.com

www.childrenscommissioner.gov.uk

www.draxe.com

www.gingerbread.org.uk

www.hiddenstrength.com

www.independent.co.uk

www.lnreview.co.uk

www.ons.gov.uk

www.telegraph.co.uk

www.theconversation.com

www.thestartingpointcentre.co.uk

www.topdoctors.co.uk

www.yougov.co.uk

Where can I find help?

Below are some telephone numbers, email addresses and websites of agencies or charities that can offer support or advice if you, or someone you know needs it.

Action for Children
www.actionforchildren.org.uk

Childline
Helpline: 0800 1111
www.childline.org.uk

Families Need Fathers
Helpline: 0300 0300 363
www.fnf.org.uk

Family Lives
Helpline: 0808 800 2222
www.familylives.org.uk

Gingerbread
Single Parent Helpline: 0808 802 0925
www.gingerbread.org.uk

ParentLine Scotland
Helpline: 08000 28 22 33
www.parentlinescotland.org.uk

The Mix
Helpline: 0808 808 4994
www.themix.org.uk

YoungMinds
Helpline: 0808 802 5544
www.youngminds.org.uk

Adoption

When a family becomes the legal guardians (adoptive parents) for a child who cannot be brought up by his or her biological parents. Couples who are infertile but wish to have a child look to adoption as an alternative. More recently, laws regarding adoption from overseas have become less strict.

Ageing population

A population whose average age is rising. This can be caused by increased life expectancy, for example following significant medical advances, or by falling birth rates, for example due to the introduction of contraception. However, the higher the proportion of older people within a population, the lower the birth rate will become due to there being fewer people of childbearing age.

Child maintenance

Usually paid by the parent who is not the primary caregiver/day-to-day carer of the child. Designed to provide financial help towards a child's everyday living costs. This can be organised through the Child Maintenance Service, but can also be agreed privately.

Civil partnership

The Civil Partnership Act 2004 (CPA) allowed LGB people the right to form legal partnerships for the first time, giving them rights comparable to those of married couples. A civil partnership can now be converted to a marriage for same-sex partners.

Cohabitation

People in an intimate relationship who live together. In the eyes of the law, cohabiting couples do not have the same rights as married couples (for example, a couple who are cohabiting do not qualify to be each other's next of kin).

Cohabiting couple

Two people who live together as a couple but are not married or in a civil partnership. Current trends suggest more couples are choosing to have children in cohabiting rather than married relationships.

Common law marriage

Many people believe that a marriage-like relationship can be established simply by cohabiting for an extended period of time. In legal terms, this is not true. Cohabitation does not lead to the same rights as marriage.

Dependent children

Usually defined as persons aged under 16, or 16 to 18 and in full-time education, who are part of a family unit and living in the household.

Divorce

The legal ending of a marriage after a permanent breakdown of the relationship. Grounds for divorce include adultery, unreasonable behaviour, separation, and desertion.

Family

A domestic group related by blood, marriage or other familial ties living together in a household. A 'traditional' or nuclear family usually refers to one in which a married heterosexual couple raise their biological children together; however, changing family structures has resulted in so-called 'non-traditional' family groups including step-families, families with adopted or foster children, single-parent families and children being raised by same-sex parents.

Lone/single parent

Someone who is raising a child alone, either due to divorce/separation, widowhood, an absent parent or due to single adoption. The majority of lone parents are women.

Marriage

When two people join together in a close and intimate union that is recognised by law. In the UK, the legal age at which you can marry is 18-years-old, or 16- to 17-years-old if you have parental consent. The Marriage (Same Sex Couples) Act 2013, which allows same-sex marriage in England and Wales, was passed by the UK Parliament in July 2013 and came into force on 13 March 2014. The Marriage and Civil Partnership (Minimum Age) Act 2022 will come into effect on Monday 27 February 2023. The Act will raise the age of marriage and civil partnership to 18 in England and Wales

Parental responsibility

When an adult has the legal right to take responsibility for the care and well-being of their child(ren) and can make important decisions about things such as food, clothing and education, this is referred to as parental responsibility. Married couples having children together automatically have this right, as do all mothers, but if the parents are unmarried the father only has parental responsibility if certain conditions are met.

Step-family

Step-families come together when people marry again or live with a new partner. This may be after the death of one parent, separation or divorce. It can also mean that children from different families end up living together for all or part of the time. One in four children has parents who get divorced and over half of their mothers and fathers will remarry or re-partner to form a step-family.

Index

A

acceptance 4

arguments 41

   see also conflict

aunts, role of 26–27

C

conflict 16, 41

D

divorce 5, 32–34, 36–37

Divorce, Dissolution and Separation Act 2020 32

donor egg families 14

E

emotional health 17

ethnicity, and household composition 8–9

extended families 3

F

family influence 16–18

family life 1–4

family structures 2–3, 5–10, 14–15

family therapy 18

fathers, nurturing parenting style 19–20

G

grandparents 4, 5

H

health and wellbeing, and family relationships 16–18

household composition 6–9

I

illegitimacy 12–13

L

LBGTQ families 14–15

life expectancy 5

lone parent families *see* single parent families

M

marriage 5

mealtimes, importance of 21–25

Mediterranean diet 24

mental health 17, 25, 37

N

nuclear family 5, 10

nurturing parenting style 19–20

P

parents, attitudes and opinions 30–31

pets 3

positive relationships 16–18

R

Relate 37

responsibility 2, 16

S

SEND 2

separation 33–35

   see also divorce

single parent families 5, 9, 10, 22

step-families 3, 5

stigmatization 12–14

stress 1–2

T

transgender parents 15

trust 4, 16

U

unconditional love 4

unmarried parents 5, 12–13